Multimodal Therapy With Children

(PGPS-73)

PERGAMON GENERAL PSYCHOLOGY SERIES

Editor: Arnold P. Goldstein, *Syracuse University*
Leonard Krasner, *SUNY, Stony Brook*

TITLES IN THE PERGAMON GENERAL PSYCHOLOGY SERIES
(Added Titles in Back of Volume)

The terms of our inspection copy service apply to all the above books. A complete catalogue of all books in the Pergamon International Library is available on request.

The Publisher will be pleased to receive suggestions for revised editions and new titles.

Multimodal Therapy With Children

Donald B. Keat II

Pergamon Press

NEW YORK • OXFORD • TORONTO • SYDNEY • FRANKFURT • PARIS

Pergamon Press Offices:

U.S.A.   Pergamon Press Inc., Maxwell House, Fairview Park,
               Elmsford, New York 10523, U.S.A.

U.K.   Pergamon Press Ltd., Headington Hill Hall,
               Oxford OX3 0BW, England

CANADA   Pergamon of Canada, Ltd., I50 Consumers Road,
               Willowdale, Ontario M2J 1P9, Canada

AUSTRALIA   Pergamon Press (Aust) Pty. Ltd., P O Box 544,
               Potts Point, NSW 2011, Australia

FRANCE   Pergamon Press SARL, 24 rue des Ecoles,
               75240 Paris, Cedex 05, France

FEDERAL REPUBLIC   Pergamon Press GmbH, 6242 Kronberg/Taunus,
OF GERMANY   Pferdstrasse 1, Federal Republic of Germany

Copyright © 1979 Pergamon Press Inc.

Library of Congress Cataloging in Publication Data

Keat, Donald B
    Multimodal therapy with children.

    (Pergamon general psychology series ; v. 73)
    1. Child psychotherapy. I. Title. [DNLM:
1. Psychotherapy--In infancy and childhood. WS350.2
K24m]
RJ504.K4 1979   618.9'28'91   78-7044
ISBN 0-08-022236-6

Printed in the United States of America

Contents

Appendices

Preface

It is now about five years that I have been involved with the multimodal approach. This comprehensive model has become a part of living for me for both personal and professional growth. The primary purpose of this book is to share this multimodal model with you.

The first milestone in the multimodal movement occurred with the publication of the book, Multimodal Behavior Therapy (1976). The editor of that book was the internationally known and acclaimed psychotherapist, Dr. Arnold A. Lazarus. I was privileged to be able to contribute two child case studies to that book. I view the current book, Multimodal Therapy With Children, as the second milestone in the multimodal Zeitgeist.

In the assembling of this book, I'd like to acknowledge several debts. First and foremost, to Arnie Lazarus. We are wedded, in a sense, by our common goal of constantly looking for effective therapeutic techniques. That is one reason why the multimodal approach is so beautiful. It doesn't matter what the theoretical background of a procedure is. The primary questions are: "Does it work?"; "Is it useful?"; "Is it an effective therapeutic strategy?"

Arnold Lazarus introduced me to these ideas at a workshop in 1973. Since that time I've used the model daily and have thus become thoroughly imbued with the variables. During the past four years, I've also had the privilege of visiting, writing, and calling Arnie in order to share ideas. The past year we've been involved in presenting workshops at numerous conventions (i.e., APA, AABT, AOA). Although I've tried to document and give him credit for most of his ideas, I'm sure that some of them have become so much a part of me that they're difficult to separate out anymore. My task has been to take his clinically innovative ideas and translate them into workable form for those of us who work primarily with children. And that's what this book is all about: an expansion and natural enlargement of the multimodal system to include applications to self-growth, children, adolescents, peers, parents, and the schools.

My second debt is to the thousands of children and families I've had professional contact with over the past 19 years. These contacts have provided a rich clinical background. I've worked in schools (i.e., Bangor,

Wilson Boro), clinics (i.e., Irving Schwartz Institute for Children and Youth, Family Guidance Center), hospitals (i.e., Philadelphia Psychiatric and Reading, Pennsylvania), and have been a consultant to numerous state and federal programs. Currently, I combine a university professorship with an active private practice in affiliation with the Psychological Associates of State College. These places, and more importantly the contacts with the professional persons and clients therein, have provided me with an immeasurable wealth of experiences. And, since we are a product of our own unbringing, I want to acknowledge the cognitive inspiration of my father who helped me to combine psychology and education in my life's work, the affective lessons of my mother who taught me the intrinsic value of caring, and the interpersonal experiences with my big sister (Kathryne) who showed that sibling interactions can be mostly positive and supportive. Finally, I thank my current family, including the five persons to whom I dedicated my last book, which is a source of perspiration (helps to keep me honest in my family recommendations) and inspiration (the joys of my own family provide many of the peak experiences in my life).

During the assembling of this book I've had the privilege of surrounding myself with some talented persons, several of whom have co-authored chapters. These people will soon be discussed in reference to the chapters they wrote with me. Most of the accuracy of the chapters' contents can be attributed to the high level skill and competency of the "happy-face" person who typed this book, Suzy Blazer Lutz.

What follows is a "common sense" sequence for the chapters.

The initial chapter presents an overview of the system and the use of the model. Many of the ideas contained therein are quoted from Arnold Lazarus' introductory remarks, which he made as moderator of our multimodal therapy panel at The American Orthopsychiatric Association meetings. In addition, I present a brief child case, some special considerations for working with children, and tie together the two synonymous acronyms (i.e., BASIC ID and HELPING) I use to work with the model.

Based upon the premise that you need to have things together well yourself before you can effectively help others, in Chapter 2 I've presented the multimodal model as a way of HELPING yourself ("if you want to"). Then Linda Leaman, an experienced child-adolescent counselor who is now completing her doctorate at Penn State, applies the model to the multimodal growth of children.

My usual stance is that accurate assessment precedes effective treatment. Therefore, before getting into actual cases, I present the model and a series of tables which summarize procedures one can use to evaluate the seven modes for your clients (Chapter 3). Then in Chapter 4 I turn to what I view as perhaps the most important variable in working with children - that is, finding out what turns them on (in the reward sense).

Next I present two classic cases which I've worked with in recent years. The child case (Chapter 5) has been terminated and the adolescent case (Chapter 6) is now down to once-a-month contact (it probably will also be terminated by the time this book is published).

Then the relatively new arena of peer helpees is explored (Chapter 7). Gains in this area can be noted on both sides: both helpers and helpees benefit.

The next natural step in the treatment sequence is to consider the home environment. Therefore, I present (Chapter 8) the HELPING model as used with parents, which is based upon another book in preparation. Then a case is given which illustrates how you can apply the multimodal approach to your family practice.

Again, based upon the assessment first then planning intervention strategies sequence, we present a classroom evaluation procedure (Classroom Ecology Schedule). The development of this scale is primarily the work of a talented person with whom I've had the pleasure of being associated for the past two years, Dick Judah. He has recently taken another position as chief psychologist at the North Central Massachusetts Mental Health Center in Fitchburg, Massachusetts. The next chapter (10) was also co-authored with an esteemed colleague, Ed Gerler, who is now a professor at North Carolina State University in Raleigh, North Carolina. In it we point out effective classroom strategies for each of the seven modes of the school environment.

Finally, Chapter 11 (again, with Dick Judah) presents a BASIC ID summary table which can serve as a basis for continued professional growth. By using this table you can develop personalized techniques to help you become a more effective therapist.

The 10 appendices are provided because they are useful. The relaxation directions (Appendix A) can be used with your child and adolescent clients. The parent education bibliography (Appendix B) can either be duplicated and given to parents for self-selection of readings or you can use the annotations to guide your recommended readings for them. The child bibliotherapy (books) and audiotherapy (tapes and records) listing (Appendix C) can be used by you for your office or clinic lending library, or to give to parents for consideration for their children. The adolescent bibliotherapy appendix (Appendix D) is both for your consideration for office books as well as for parents or the adolescents themselves. Appendix E presents a multimodal classification for part of a commercially available program (DUSO); it was developed by Barbara Green and Nancy Gerber. The contents of Appendix F give you a classroom exercise which you can present to a teacher for actual use in the classroom. It was developed by a teacher, Barbara Arevalo, for her classroom in Central America. The final four appendices (G, H, I, J) have at least two uses: one, for your own use if you want to explore the procedures further and incorporate them into your technique armamentarium and two, as a module for a class experience in therapy procedures course.

The multimodal therapy approach provides a comprehensive model for assessment methods and treatment strategies. The contents of this book present my current thinking on what I'm finding to be effective. I hope that you will find the multimodal system to be as useful as I have.

Donald B. Keat II
University Park, PA

1 Multimodal Therapy: An Overview

The current Zeitgeist in psychology is the "multimodal movement." This balanced approach represents the new way of conducting effective therapy. What the approach represents is a comprehensive way of first identifying problems and then utilizing effective intervention strategies in order to ameliorate the client's condition. Due to the fact that it is really the techniques which help our clients, this approach can also be labeled "pragmatic technical eclecticism." If you use this approach, your results will be more rapid and long lasting.

THE MULTIMODAL MODEL

In the multimodal approach there are seven interactive modalities which we investigate and then we intervene where necessary. The modes are interactive in that change in one mode can have effects in other zones. The seven modes are Behavior, Affect (feelings, emotions), Sensation, Imagery, Cognition, Interpersonal relationships, and Drugs-Diet. Taking the first letter of each of the seven cited modes, the acronym "BASIC ID" (Lazarus, 1976) is used to represent this approach and as a convenient way of remembering the seven zones.

In the process of understanding these modalities and explaining them to clients, I have found several analogies to be useful. You can vary your

---

* Much of the material in this chapter is based upon the initial overview remarks made by Arnold A. Lazarus (Ph.D) as moderator of a multimodal behavior therapy workshop at The 54th Annual Meeting of The American Orthopsychiatric Association, New York City, April 14, 1977. Other workshop contributors were Barry M. Brown (M.D.) and Donald B. Keat II (Ph.D.).

explanation and use all four, select your favorite one, or develop your own. The first analogy is to the seven notes (A, B, C, D, E, F, G) of the natural (no sharps or flats) music scale. Musicians, by using combinations of the seven main notes A to G (plus five other sharps and/or flats comprising the complete 12 tones of a musical scale), can compose and play beautiful ballads or hard rock. With these same notes, a person can play chopsticks or Bach. So the therapist is confronted with the seven musical notes of personality (i.e., BASIC ID) and orchestrates his/her therapy composition by the armamentaria of procedures used in each mode.

Another interesting comparison is to use the colors of the rainbow, that is "BIG ORVY," or the seven colors of Blue, Indigo, Green, Orange, Red, Violet, and Yellow. This is an acronym which I've carried for close to 30 years in order to remember the seven basic colors (BASIC ID = Colors of Personality).

A useful way of conceptualizing the multimodal approach is to think in terms of a seven-geared car (some cars now have five-on-the-floor, plus reverse, so seven will probably soon be with us) or a bike with seven gears (somewhere between the five and 10 commonly used). The idea here would be to select a mode to work in first (e.g., presenting concern with acting-out Behavior). After effective procedures have helped in this mode, then you would want to shift into another mode and work in as many modes as is necessary to achieve positive results. The BASIC ID premise is, of course, that if you don't cover all seven of the modes, you are doing a half-baked incomplete job. People will relapse! If you don't deal with all seven, "it's like an earthworm that regenerates - let one segment that's untouched, it's going to start regenerating" (Lazarus, 1977). The reward, of course, is longer lasting results.

The final useful way of conceptualizing this approach is that of using the BASIC ID approach as a type of lens, viewpiece, or pair of eyeglasses through which you zoom in on the modes which you are investigating in order to determine where to intervene. The BASIC ID is the head-profile or compass which guides your gaze into these "Pillars of Personality."

AND BEYOND

But something is missing from the BASIC ID. "The something that is missing is Environment, Culture" (Lazarus, 1977). And you need to take cognizance of that as a clinician. This is especially true when working with children because there are two major life environments which need to be included: school and home. You could elect to enlarge the acronym and use BASIC IDEAL in which E represents Educational or school pursuits, A stands for significant Adults in the child's life (parents, teachers, relatives), and L means to Learn the client's culture. But I prefer instead to expand the seven pillars to encompass these two important life influences. Therefore, as outlined previously (Keat, 1976a), the S is expanded to cover the school environment and the interpersonal relations mode is broadened to include both family (especially parents) considerations as well as the broader environmental (e.g., community) contexts.

YOUR ROLE

The multimodal approach is conceived as a training enterprise. We are "teachers, trainers, educators" (Lazarus, 1977). In this role you model; you show; you instruct. People try and imitate you. They try on your way first, but then they tailor it to their own needs. That is, they personalize it to fit their style.

THE MULTIMODAL APPROACH

What do you do when you first meet a client? "When you meet a client you take a history. You'll enter into a relationship. Formulate hypotheses" (Lazarus, 1977). During (if you and client reel comfortable in your taking notes) or after the interview you write the BASIC ID letters downward on the left hand side of the page and see what you can put in each category under the problem heading (See Table 1-1 in this chapter, plus the profiles in Chapters 2, 4, 5, 6, 7, and 10). Then either during the session or at the end you can summarize your findings for your client and outline what you think might be done in some of the problem areas. Before the next session you then figure out other intervention strategies and outline questions you may need to ask to fill in the gaps of relevant material.

Then you have developed a complete BASIC ID for your client. This will evolve with each contact. It doesn't matter where you put the problem in the model; fit it somewhere. Certain ones are clear (A = anxiety, anger) while others are more debatable (e.g., assertiveness under behavior, or affect). But put it in. And then the main therapeutic task is to determine what can be DONE? What can you do to ameliorate the problems, concerns, troubles you are presented with. The difficult task for the clinician is usually not to determine what's wrong (see Chapters 3 and 9), but to determine what will be the most effective way of helping the person with his/her concern(s). This is what most of the rest of this book is about (see especially the cases as well as Chapter 11).

The following example is briefly presented to show how you might use this approach with a child. More detailed cases will be presented in subsequent chapters (i.e., 5, 6). This case involved an 11-year-old boy from an intact family with a younger sister. The primary presenting problems were: inappropriate expression of anger (biting teacher), low self-image (partially due to ridicule), mistaken ideas (he agreed with all 20 ideas from the Lazarus and Fay, 1975 list), and lack of friends. The abridged illustrative profile follows.

Table 1-1
Multimodal Profile for Fred

Mode	Problem	Proposed Treatment
B	Jobs around house	Behavioral contracting
A	Anger Anxiety	Reprogramming expression Relaxation training
S	Music interest	Enhance, training
I	Low self-image	IALAC training
C	Mistaken ideas	Rational emotive
IP	Lacks friends	Friendship training
D	Eating habits	Nutrition discussions, readings

Initially, the most important concern was his anger. The school was upset because of the teacher biting incident. Therefore, the first method of intervention was in the affective mode. We worked on physical (directed muscular activity), verbal expression (words to say), as well as things to do in imagery (without acting on them). A multimodal approach within the affect mode was also used in relaxation training in that he was given a child tape (Keat, 1977, Tape 2) which describes relaxation as breathing and learning to tense-relax various muscle groups (sensation mode), calling forth appropriate calm scenes (imagery), and repeating relaxing sentences (cognitive zone) to oneself. This type of second-order multimodal analysis will be discussed in more detail shortly.

In the sensation-school mode he had great strength. It is important to accentuate skills and not to belabor deficiencies. Therefore, special arrangements were made for him to get supplementary musical training outside of the school. In addition, we formed a musical group which rehearsed monthly for which he wrote arrangements and took conducting responsibilities. Both the therapist and one of his sons participated in this group. Low self-image is a common difficulty in children. He was trained in I am Loveable and Capable (IALAC) (Simon, 1973) self-perceptions as well as dealing with his fear of ridicule. An example of this fear will be discussed subsequently under second-order multimodal analysis.

Friendship training was instituted because he was a scapegoated child. During sessions, we talked about where to meet (e.g., musical groups), how to greet (what to say as participants came to the door), and how to keep friends (by being considerate, don't put them down for mistakes, etc.).

The diet mode was of relatively little concern but we did discuss nutrition and we read certain publications (e.g., U.S. Department of Agriculture, 1975). Also, the behavioral mode was dealt with by the commonly used procedure of contracting in which agreed upon house jobs were rewarded.

From this brief abridged profile it can be seen that the first zone of intervention is generally the presenting problem(s). With children, the usual presenting modes are: behavior, affect, school, interpersonal relations.

After one assesses the problems and figures out relevant treatment strategies, one can move into other modes in which there can be constructive intervention.

Sometimes after you have taken the history, established a working relationship, developed the BASIC ID program which relates the problems to what you are going to do about them, and worked therapeutically with your client, things may not be resolved as anticipated. What you can do then is to run through a "second-order BASIC ID" (Lazarus, 1977). Within the model, you have started with a global view of personality (first-order BASIC ID), but then you can look at any of those items on that profile and put them on a second-order BASIC ID.

In order to personalize this, let's use an example which most of us have or could have experienced, i.e., ridicule. Initially, ridicule could be placed under Imagery (an attack of one's self-image). The following table summarizes (as in Fred's case of scapegoating) the modal questions (e.g., What's your behavior, feeling, etc.?), and the client's answers to the question of responding to ridicule (Lazarus, 1977).

Table 1-2
Second-Order BASIC ID
(Imagery: Ridicule)

Mode (What's your behavior, etc.)	Response (answer)
Behavior	Strong withdrawal
Affect	Absolute rage
Sensation	Surging heat
Imagery	Attack, kill
Cognition	Mother was right
Interpersonal relations	Utter rejection
Drugs	Not applicable

In this situation you could start with "mother was right" by using the Gestalt empty chair technique (Perls, 1969) with dialogue between mother and son and the child refuting the mother. Then use imagery by getting him to attack and then face the consequences (to acquire the feeling that it's not worth it). In the cognitive mode you can use the "so what if" procedure (Lazarus, 1971) in which you say to yourself "so what if they make fun of me, I won't let it bother me." For the interpersonal difficulty you can use friendship training (see Chapter 8). In this approach the person is trained in where to meet, greet (what to say), and how to keep friends. The final category (keeping) is, of course, the most difficult and involves such things as developing a wide range of interests, the nature of reciprocal relationships, and so forth. By looking at one of the mode's problems by this type of second-order analysis, you can sometimes more effectively lessen the difficulty.

How can you use this profile? I use it as a personal chart for the child or adolescent for planning therapy. With parents or teachers you can share the chart. Chapter 8 describes how to do this with parents.

This multimodal profile represents a seven-step plan for persons. With your enthusiasm and encouragement, you can help them to change.

HELPING CLIENTS

The BASIC ID model is fine for professionals who have training in psychology. Indeed, it can even provide an entré into certain therapeutic circles where the approach is based upon the id, ego, superego conceptualization.

For lay persons, however, who are outside of the lingo and catch-words of our profession, this acronym did not seem to make much sense. Therefore, I asked myself, what is the core of what you do? The answer came as I was helping children and parents. In addition, in what are most adults who are concerned about children interested? They're interested in helping children. Therefore, I adapted the same seven areas into another acronym - H E L P I N G. Using the same seven modes, my task was to fit the modes into this word. The results are shown in Table 1-3.

Table 1-3
Multimodal Evolution

Letter	BASIC ID	HELPING	Letter	
	Modes	Modes		
B	Behavior	Guidance of A, B, Cs	G	
A	Affect	Emotions - feelings	E	
S	Sensation-school	Learning - school	L	
				→ HELPING
I	Imagery	Imagination-interests	I	
C	Cognition	Need to know - think	N	
I	Interpersonal relations	People-personal relationships	P	
D	Drugs-diet	Health	H	

This HELPING acronym has proven to be particularly useful in communicating the concepts to parents (Chapter 8), peers (Chapter 7), and in dealing with adults about self-growth (Chapter 2). The modes remain the same. It all depends on to whom you're trying to communicate the concepts.

SPECIAL CONSIDERATIONS FOR CHILDREN

Lazarus (1976) has eloquently stated the multimodal case for adults. The purpose of this book is to develop the concepts and present techniques for therapists interested in working with children.

Therefore, certain differences should be kept in mind. Play is the work of the child and forms a major vehicle for the relationship with children. Ginott (1961, p. 51) has stated that "the child's play is his talk and toys are his words." The child therapist needs to be familiar with the media of play and the use of toys in the child's world. It is important to develop your own play bag (Keat, 1974a).

Communication, therefore, will tend to be different. Until the child becomes more verbal and can relate as a mature adult, he/she may use drawing, puppets, and a variety of games to relate to and communicate with you. This makes child therapy challenging and alive.

Another major area is the use of bibliotherapy (see Appendix C). This means the use of stories therapeutically. The trick here is to select meaningful stories; Dick Gardner (a child psychiatrist) has helped us in this area in recent years (e.g., Gardner, 1972).

The final consideration I want to mention in this initial chapter is the importance of working with significant adults in the child's life. Therefore, I've included separate chapters on both home and school interventions.

The two most important questions you need to keep answering as a multimodal child therapist are: How can I HELP this child? and Is what I'm doing effective?

THE REST OF THE BOOK

What is to follow should help you in this pursuit of being an effective multimodal child therapist. Based upon the stance that you need to be together yourself before you can effectively help others, I've written the first part of the growth chapter (Linda Leaman applies the growth model to children in Chapter 2). Then the premise that insightful assessment precedes effective treatment is acted upon and two chapters are presented which deal with individual assessment (Chapter 3) and turning children on (Chapter 3 and 4). The BASIC ID model is applied to a child case (Chapter 5) and an adolescent situation (Chapter 6). The importance of considering peer helpers is delineated (Chapter 7), then the multimodal approach to working with parents is outlined (Chapter 8). Based on the assessment-intervention paradigm, an ecology schedule (Chapter 9) is presented (with Dick Judah) prior to considering multimodal education (Chapter 10, written with Ed Gerler). Finally, a summary chapter will tie it all together (Chapter 11) so that you can effectively use the multimodal approach in child therapy.

2 Multimodal Growth: Helping Yourself and Children

Multimodal growth means that all people can benefit from considering possible ways of HELPING themselves. Although not espousing a lengthy personal analysis, it does seem important for persons whose job is to help others to be working toward some personal self-improvement. This growth can be of benefit not only to yourself, but also to those persons you are proposing to help.

The persons you are called upon to help who will benefit are not only the children to be described in the second half of this chapter, but also the adults (e.g., parents, teachers, school administrators) with whom you work. By having experienced multimodal growth personally, you will be in a better position in HELPING them down a similar path.

HELPING YOURSELF

In a certain sense personal growth might be likened to making a New Year's Resolution. You can view this as a time for optimism. It can be a time for self-renewal, a time to believe that you can have some control over your future, that you can make resolutions which can be realized, and that you can change for the better. Remember, you can change if you want to.

There are some basic steps which you can take in approaching these goals. First, pick at least one thing from one of the seven modes and work on it until you improve in the selected area. Secondly, teach yourrself what you need to know in order to develop the skill (e.g., read a book or chapter about it). Thirdly, practice the skill in everyday life situations so that you can gain competence in it. Fourthly, move on to something else in the process of HELPING yourself.

In creating your personality orchestration, just as in the seven main modes

---

*   This chapter was co-authored by Linda J. Leaman

of the musical scale discussed in Chapter 1, the acronym HELPING will be used. Table 2-1 presents some suggested possible areas under each mode. These areas will be briefly discussed in the mode-to-mode sequence with the hope of precipitating some ideas for your personal growth.

Table 2-1
Multimodal Growth - HELPING Yourself

Modality	Task, Skill, Concern	Training
Health	Overweight Smoking Alcohol Physical conditioning	Diet Count, Saturation Monitor, Club (e.g., AA) Aerobics
Emotions - Feelings	Joy Anxiety Anger	Fun training Relax, Meditation Training Pre-programming
Learning - Sensory	Visual aesthetics Aural appreciation Sexual skills Kinesthetic abilities	Art appreciation Music listening Sex education Dance, Yoga
Personal Relationships	Getting along with others Listening and hearing Time with children	Friendship training Communication training HELPING child
Imagery - Interests	Self-concept Become interesting Train imagery	IALAC awareness RSC survey Fire drills
Need to Know	Irrational ideas Decision making How to study	Rational thinking training Problem-solving practice Study skills
Guidance of A, B, C's	Time use Lack assertiveness General behavioral skills	Scheduling Assertiveness training Behavior rehearsal

Health

Your health should be an almost daily concern. As adults, we should be able to monitor and attain an optimum level of functioning through appropriate dietary intake and rest-activity schedules. Personally, I've taken courses and read books (e.g., Robinson, 1972) in the area of diet therapy.. I try to eat as natural a diet as possible for breakfast and lunch, and to eat a balanced meal (e.g., meats, vegetables, bread, milk) in the evening. I often skip lunch two or three times a week both because of appointments as well as the feeling of enhanced functioning in the afternoon when my body is not called upon to process foods. My wife has extended this to fasting one day a week (Cott, 1975).

Another nutritionist who provides useful information is Fredericks (1976). In his recent book he outlines a BAMBY plan for eating (Bran, And Multiple vitamins and Minerals, B complex vitamins, Yogurt). Indeed, certain foods, such as salt and sugar (Keat & Guerney, 1978), should be avoided. Yudkin (1972) makes an extremely strong case against the ingestion of sweets. Even in songs we can hear this plea made. For example, the words from part of the bridge of "You Belong to Me" state: "Don't eat sweets. You'll get a pain and ruin your tum-tum."

In the concern area of smoking too much, Lazarus (1976) has outlined a multimodal approach to this "habit." He suggests a four-mode intervention, which includes altering the behavioral conditions under which smoking is to occur (e.g., "Begin by limiting your smoking to the first 15 minutes of any hour"). He also suggests simultaneously attending to affective elements ("When you feel anxious try to employ the differential relaxation you have just learned instead of reaching for a cigarette"). In addition, a simple sensory exercise is often helpful - for example, inhaling an ammonia compound while smoking so as to develop a distinctly negative sensory association. Imagery can be effective in two distinct ways. First, modify the positive imagery ("Instead of identifying with Bogart, picture yourself telling him that in the light of recent medical evidence, anyone who smokes is asking for trouble"). Then try introducing aversive imagery ("When you light up a cigarette try to think of scenes that literally nauseate you") (Lazarus, 1976, pp. 92-93).

Too much drinking and even alcoholism are rather common concerns in our society. There are a variety of ways in which you can attempt to decrease intake. For example, you can either try to avoid such drinking situations or, if in one, use glass-in-hand behavior (with orange juice or soda) in order to meet the social demands of the situation. Maintain the imagery of being okay despite not going along with the group, and tell yourself that you are a superior person for not imbibing.

In a balanced approach to health, physical exercise is an important component. Americans have become enamored with positive addiction (Glasser, 1976); on almost any street you can see persons walking, waddling, jogging, or even running. Indeed, the popularity of such books as the ones on aerobics (Cooper, 1968, 1970; Cooper & Cooper, 1972) reflects the great interest in physical exercise. Almost anyone can develop a program to meet his or her physical needs.

Emotions-Feelings

Life is a mixture of a lot of emotions with variations from feelings of highs (joy, happiness) to being low and blue (sad, depressed). One way in which you can tune in to the good feelings in life is what I call "fun training." That is, by just cataloging and becoming aware of some of the things that turn you on, you can then better appreciate and enhance your enjoyment of them while you're doing them. For example, some things that I enjoy are working with children, listening to and playing music, playing with and putting my children to bed, going to the movies (especially ones like The Return of the Pink Panther, or Young Frankenstein), dancing, shopping, certain TV programs, reading, and playing games. What do you do for fun? When is the last time you did it? Get on with it and contract with yourself to get more enjoyment out of life!

A major concern for many persons is overwhelming anxiety. We all experience anxiety; in its positive form it can spur us on to productive moments. But it can also be debilitating and interfere with our functioning. When this is the case, relaxation training is the most appropriate antidote. By learning how to relax deeply, you can gain control over your feelings of anxiety. There are a variety of books on the topic (e.g., Gutwirth, 1968; Jacobsen, 1962; Walker, 1975), but one of the easiest ways to acquire these skills is simply by listening to cassette tapes. There are a variety of such tapes available for adults, but the ones I find most suitable are the ones by Lazarus (1970, 1975). Some persons find that Transcendental Meditation (TM) is a useful adjunct to their lives. For those of us who would rather do it ourselves, there are many books (e.g., Bloomfield, Cain, Jaffe & Kory, 1975; Hemingway, 1975) that describe the process, but relatively few that get into the "how to" (Akins & Nurnberg, 1976; LeShan, 1974). And if you are really into it, why not attend the TM introductory lectures to see if it's for you? In case it is, pay your fee, buy yourself a white handkerchief (if you don't have one, that is), three different pieces of fresh fruit, and a small bunch of fresh flowers. Then meet with your instructor several times, get your mantra, and program two 20-minute time slots into your morning and afternoon for meditation.

The final emotion I want to discuss is that of anger. We all experience anger. The trick is to learn to pre-program yourself so that you can vent your angry feelings in such a way that no one gets hurt (yourself or others). It is useful to think in terms of at least three ways in which to dissipate angry feelings. The first one is physical. What can I do to expend the anger I feel? Such things as "directed muscular activity" (DMA) can be effective - e.g. pound a pillow or slam your fist into your hand. The second outlet can be verbal. What do you say when you are angry? Be careful where you say it, or go into the bathroom, turn on the shower (radio or anything else available) and scream! The third mode you can use is imagery. In your "minds-eye" you can make believe you're telling off the person who upset you, or doing something to someone you dislike. It's only a make-believe game, one which you won't act on, so take license and do whatever you like. Much anger can be dealt with by what you tell yourself about what happened. For example, if you're standing in the hall leaning against the wall talking to someone and a person walks into you, your irritation will probably dissipate when you turn around and see that the person is blind. Another useful procedure for lessening your anger (both toward yourself and others) will be discussed under the "Need to Know" section of this chapter.

Learning-Sensory

The area of learning basically means to open yourself up to experiencing a broader range of feelings in the sensory area (i.e., visual, auditory, olfactory, tactile, gustatory, and kinesthetic). In the zone of visual aesthetics, you can try to be sensitive to various types of pictures, or you might just want to become more aware of your surroundings and appreciate such things as nature (trees, flowers, sunsets).

A second major area to become tuned into is that of music. Personally, this is my strong area (auditory), and one to which I am extremely sensitive. For me, this involvement is on a performance level and has been extremely rewarding. But you can also become sensitized on a listening level so that you can glean enjoyment from records. With such auditory pursuits, you can broaden some of your joys in life.

The third area in which you might want to enhance your personal functioning is that of sexual skills. The sense of touch is one which can be developed by trial and error and open communication with your partner. Or you can get into some of the variety of self-help sex manuals (Comfort, 1972; Kaplan, 1975). When used constructively, such sources can provide you with an awareness of certain erogenous zones of which you may not have been aware before. Then you can personalize them to suit your needs.

The final area to be discussed in this mode is that of kinesthetic skills. Although these abilities have to do mostly with the sense of balance, herein we broaden the concept to include most large muscle movement activities. Dance classes can be fun, provide exercise, and provide extrinsic rewards if you do it well enough. If you are interested in stretching your muscles, learning how to breathe appropriately, and perhaps becoming aware of some of the Eastern philosophical underpinnings, then yoga may be for you. There are a variety of books which can fill you in (e.g., Hittleman, 1969; Lysebeth, 1971). And many communities have either yoga schools or classes established in public school facilities.

Personal Relationships

Learning to get along well with others takes a lot of practice. Friendship training approaches need to be related to the adult level. For example, where can you meet people? (e.g., Ellis, 1965). Secondly, how do you greet persons so that the conversation can flow easily, and what can you say in order to engage someone in meaningful dialogue. Finally, consider how you can become an interesting person - that is, a person with a variety of topics which you can talk about and interests which you can share. Showing concern for others is a good way to be a friend.

One of the major blocks to effective interpersonal relationships is difficulty in, or breakdowns in, communication. Being a good listener, and really hearing and responding in a meaningful way, can aid your communication. Most of us, of course, have had communication skills training and therefore probably have this avenue functioning adequately, but it takes constant work and practice to keep your skills sharp. A periodic refresher course or book on the topic (e.g., Danish & Hauer, 1973) might be helpful.

With children, either your own or those with whom you work, the HELPING approach as discussed in Chapter 1 and Chapter 8 should be useful. As a parent or a counselor, quality time alone with a child is necessary in order to cement your positive relationship. This involvement, in turn, can be one of the most rewarding experiences in your life. You both can gain reciprocally from the positive time shared together in your interaction.

Imagery-Interests

The mental images we have of ourselves are the basis for how we feel about ourselves. In order to develop a self-concept of I am Loveable and Capable (IALAC) (Simon, 1973), you need to learn to cope with daily stresses and to stop the self-put-downs. You also need to inoculate yourself against the criticisms of others. One way you can do this is to give yourself the assignment of "stop putting yourself down." Become aware of how often you do this (i.e., monitor your own behavior) and then consciously attempt to lessen the number of times that you make critical self-statements. Your self-feelings are, in essence, the sum of your self-statements. Therefore, try to build up your positive self-statements. The old adage, "self-praise stinks," is one of the myths of a previous generation. The way to a more positive self-image is to tell yourself good things about yourself (don't wait for others to do it).

As mentioned in the previous mode under friendship training, one way to keep friends is to become more interesting. One way of doing this is to survey your areas of interest. Take an inventory such as the reward survey (to be discussed in Chapter 4) and determine what turns you on. Are there any gaps in your interests which you could beef-up in order to make yourself more interesting? Tabulate your interests, develop the ones you are attracted to, try to enlarge your scope of knowledge, and be prepared to listen and to talk about topics which are initiated.

The final topic in this mode is the training of your imagery. Most of us really have better pictures in our minds than we give ourselves credit for. By becoming sensitive to our "mind's-eye" pictures, we can enhance the power of our imagery. One way in which you can check your current level of imagery is to take a quick imagery test (Lazarus, 1978). Once you have delineated your functioning imagery level, then you can decide whether your current level is useful. If it is, then you can utilize what we call "fire drills" in which you rehearse in imagery what you are going to do or say. For example, you are about to make a presentation to a P.T.A. or a convention. In your "mind's-eye" you practice how you are going to make your entrance, whether you are going to stand up or sit down, what your first words will be, and so forth. By the use of such covert rehearsal, we can enhance our actions, and verbal delivery so that we can be more effective.

Need to Know

This mode is really concerned with the cognitions or the self-sentences which we tell ourselves. As Epictetus said in the first century A.D.: "People are disturbed not by things, but by the views which they take of them." This quote represents a basic truism in which an event happens at point A (e.g., criticism) and the reaction at point C (e.g., anger or defensiveness) is not a result of only what happened at point A, but mainly of the beliefs, thoughts, and attitudes which the person tells himself at point B. An extremely useful way that I have found to work on these self sentences is to attempt to lessen my own "musturbation" (Ellis & Harper, 1975). Musturbation represents the musts, shoulds, and oughts which we lay on ourselves and others. For example, you may find it useful to try out the following steps in lessening self-musturbation.

1. Identify the musts, shoulds, and oughts which you lay on yourself and/or others. For example, "I must do everything perfectly" (instead of "I made another mistake; I'm a fallible human being"). Another example might be, "You should have been on time for lunch" (instead of "It would have been more considerate if you were on time").

2. Ask yourself if these self/other expectations are realistic. If your answer is "yes," then pursue your aspirations with renewed vigor (and hopefully with some success). In case you answered "no," then you will have freed yourself of some "excess baggage" and your "anger barometer" should not boil over as often. You'll probably enjoy yourself and others more - remember first to identify the irrational or mistaken idea (e.g., musturbation). Then figure out a more positive sentence as done above. Work and practice in order to internalize these new and more rational sentences. After you practice disputing your mistaken ideas for several weeks, you will be on the road to coping more successfully.

We are constantly being faced with choices in our daily living. How well or poorly we deal with making these decisions has an influence on the quality of our lives. The nature of our choices varies from relatively small ones (e.g., what to eat for breakfast) to those of greater magnitude (e.g., job-career). Choices are a part of life and how well we handle them is the key issue. Remember, for both yourselves and the children with whom you work, having a voice in the choice is very important. If we have something to say about our destiny, we are usually much more accepting of it. In cases where decisions are imposed upon us from someplace else we become resistant.

In order to make choices and solve problems in a more consistent fashion, a common sense sequence can be followed. Although some people may do this naturally, most of us can benefit from having an outline to follow in order to be more effective. After you use this sequence several times, it should become a "common sense" part of your problem-solving style.

1. Define. In order to delineate just what the decision or problem is, you need to define as specifically as possible just what you want to do.

2. Discuss. Next, the involved persons need to discuss the decision to be made or problem to be solved in order to get out feelings and experiences about it. This step is necessary to bring to light each person's feelings and ideas about the particular decision or problem.

3. Brainstorm. "Brainstorming" is an effective procedure to generate possible decison choices or alternative solutions to problems. After you generate possible ideas, you will have a better perspective on the choice to be made.

4. Evaluate. This step means to attempt to decide which possible plan or solution to the problem is the best one for the moment - that is, the one that meets the most needs of the persons involved or of the situation requiring action.

5. Implement. This step means to work out a way to put the decision or problem solution into action. This is the "doing" step and represents the trying out of the decision or problem-solving behaviors.

6. Outcome. The major question which you need to ask here is "How did it work out?" This evaluation then provides grist for the decision mill the next time a similar problem is raised.

The final area to be discussed under this mode is that of self-improvement in general study skills. These are basic skills which are necessary for effective work in the educational system and include such things as organizing your time (scheduling), taking notes, reading better and faster, studying texts, taking examinations, writing papers, and so forth. There are basically two ways to deal with this. One is to purchase a "How to Study" book (e.g., Morgan & Deese, 1969) and do it yourself. Or you can enroll in a course and have the added benefit of external motivation and structuring in the process of learning these basic skills.

Guidance of Acts, Behaviors, and Consequences
(A, B, C's)

Guidance of your own acts and behaviors as well as the related consequences is the key to your overt behavioral impressions. One thing which commonly comes to the fore is use of time. You all know that the busiest persons seem to be the ones who do the most and get the most done. The organization of your time seems to be the key issue. This involves scheduling your time, making every hour count, working during your prime time (e.g., my morning hours are generally more productive), and allocating your time so that you can meet your commitments.

The final two topics in Table 2-1 will be tied together because behavior rehearsal is a common component of assertiveness training (AT). The following steps can be a useful 'sequence in learning to be more assertive. For more details, see such sources as Alberti and Emmons (1974), Fensterheim and Baer (1975), and Lange and Jakubowski (1976). The key in assertiveness is not to be a passive Caspar Milquetoast or come on aggressively as King Kong, but to function assertively somewhere in the middle. Again, BALANCE is the key concept. Steps in AT:

1. Identify the situation that needs attention. This can be something such as the inability to say "no" to unreasonable requests.

2. Help yourself to accept personal rights and to modify any irrational ideas which you have. An example is believing that if I say "no" I will hurt the requestor's feelings.

3. Present the situation for both "mind practice" and "behavior rehearsal." In mind practice you imagine yourself saying "no" in the selected situation. During behavior rehearsal, you practice the behavior with someone else as a prelude to actually doing it. If you can locate a person who is a good model for AT, then he/she can reverse roles with you and show you how they might do it. Then you can again switch roles and try out the modeled behavior for size.

4. Try it out. The next step after you're ready would be to try out your new assertive behavior in an in vivo situation - say "no" to a request that you do something when you're already overbooked.

5. Check it out. Evaluate how your assertiveness worked. How did it go? What would you change the next time? Then develop some alternatives for handling the saying of "no" in future encounters.

SUMMARY: YOU CAN IF YOU WANT TO

In HELPING yourself the initial goal is to target at least one of the things you want to improve. Then go ahead and work on it until you have improved in the selected skill area. After you feel comfortable with that mode, go on to something else in another mode. And keep on going in the process of HELPING yourself. The only person who has no room for improvement is a dead one. Therefore, get on with it. Remember, you can if you want to.

HELPING CHILDREN

Now that we have presented ways in which you can enhance your personal growth, we shall delineate ways in which you can similarly help children. Learning coping and self-enhancement skills is important in every child's development. The first part of the following section examines the concept of multimodal therapy as a growth model. Some implications for affective education are also suggested. The remainder of the chapter provides methods and skills that can be used in HELPING children.

We are just beginning to recognize that for too long we have assumed that we "naturally" learn what might be termed "coping skills." Whether in the schools or in a private or clinical setting, we are realizing that those of us in the helping professions are sorely pressed to meet society's demands (Guerney, Stollak, & Guerney, 1971; Hersch, 1969). Even though the field is expanding rapidly, we seem to be unable to meet the needs of all those who seek our services. At the same time, assertiveness training courses, consciousness raising groups, yoga classes, and a variety of popular self-help books and similar self-enrichment programs are spreading in popularity as we seek to enrich our lives. All of this attesting to the fact that many of us, at least, have not "naturally" learned coping and self-enhancement skills. And yet we often neglect to identify and teach systematically to children those skills that we know will both enhance their lives and give them the skills to cope with and enhance their future.

As described by Lazarus (1976), the multimodal framework can be used to eliminate maladaptive behaviors and also to teach new skills in areas where behavioral deficits exist. It is in this sense that multimodal therapy is a growth model. Although he does not view it as a theoretical system, Lazarus states that the model may be "viewed as 'actualization,' 'growth,' or 'educational' rather than as one based upon disease analogies, medicine, or pathology" (p. 5).

In discussing a multidimensional view of actualization counseling and psychotherapy, Brammer and Shostrom (1968) state that:

> Psychological growth has several general, underlying principles. Growth is progressive and cumulative; that is, it moves by steps and through stages. Growth is integrative and disintegrative; that is, growth is a building- and fitting-together process as well as a tearing-down process. (p. 86)

They further suggest that psychological growth "depends upon the twin principles of maturation and learning" (p. 86). Thus, growth is seen as a process within the context of maturation that requires the "unlearning" of some behaviors and the acquisition of new, more self-enhancing behaviors. Rogers (1951) views this process as directional. In discussing the individual's striving to actualize and enhance, he suggests that the individual "moves in the direction of limited expansion through growth" (p. 488). He sees this growth as including an increase in the person's ability to cope with and adapt to life situations.

Certainly anyone could benefit from a decrease in maladaptive behaviors and an increase in adaptive, fulfilling behaviors. In order to function maximally, we need to have a whole repertoire of behaviors. Within the multimodal approach, these behaviors can be thought of as skills. Ellis (1969) argues that "teaching, skill training, and the giving of homework assignments are among the most effective forms of counseling" (p. 38). The efficacy of teaching coping and enrichment skills is being reported by many researchers (e.g., Authier, Gustafson, Guerney, & Kasdorf, 1975; Vogelsong, 1975).

In order to teach these skills, an increasing number of authors are proposing that psychological practitioners make a shift from the medical model of diagnosis and treatment to an educational model. Guerney, Stollak, and Guerney (1971) discuss the implications of this shift and point out its preventive nature. Such an approach would focus on the "teaching of personal and interpersonal attitudes and skills which the individual can apply to solve present and future psychological problems and to enhance his satisfaction with life" (p. 2). They suggest that skills such as "recognizing and expressing feelings" might be taught. Guerney (1977) further delineates four main aspects of skills training:

> (a) teaching them what it is they need to know (providing the rationale); (b) establishing the appropriate life-experience they need to elicit such behavior (providing practice); (c) helping them perfect their skills (providing supervision); and (d) increasing the use of skills in appropriate everyday-life situations (fostering generalization). (p. 26)

Multimodal behavior therapy offers a broad range of modalities within which various skill areas can be identified. Lazarus (1976) describes man as a "thinking, feeling, sensing, imagining, behaving, interrelating creature who is also biochemical." All of these modalities are interrelated and interact with each other so that by dealing with one, others are affected, but each needs to be dealt with directly. Thus, it would seem that multimodal behavior therapy has important implications for areas such as affective education. Many affective education programs focus almost exclusively on the affective domain and pay little attention to the other modalities. Keat (1974), in discussing a guide to affective curriculum materials, proposes activities and materials in many of the modalities. Multimodal behavior therapy provides a logical framework upon which to develop an affective education program. Such a program would deal systematically with each of the modalities and be comprehensive in its approach.

Whether in an affective education approach (see Chapter 10) or in individual counseling, the use of the term "skills" implies that the skills would continue to show improvement in follow-up studies due to increased practice. Vogelsong (1975), for example, has found some evidence that communication between mothers and adolescent daughters continued to improve six months after they had been taught relationship enhancement skills. In viewing the multimodal model as a growth model, we would expect this effect to be even greater since all of the modalities are systematically developed.

The purpose of most of the remainder of this chapter is to identify certain skill areas within each of the modalities and to suggest various methods that might be used in learning and teaching these skills. The diagram and accompanying explanations are not meant to be an exhaustive listing of all the possibilities. Rather it is intended to give readers a variety of examples of skills and methods that can be adapted by counselors, educators, and psychological practitioners in individual and group work, and with children as well as adolescents. Whether in a broader conceptualization of multimodal education or in working with all of the modalities in an individual approach, multimodal therapy offers us an opportunity to provide children with an armamentarium of skills to be used in coping with problems and in providing a basis for self-enhancement and growth.

The following section is divided into seven categories corresponding to each of the modalities (see Table 2-2). Within each section headings are used that suggest both skill areas and methods.

Table 2-2
Multimodal Growth: HELPING Children

Modality	Skills	Methods
Health	Diet	Nutritional information

Emotions-
Feelings
	Awareness and appropriate
	    expression of feelings
	Joy attainment
		Relationship enhancement
		    programs
		Fun training

Learning - Sensory	Auditory appreciation Motor coordination Relaxation Study skills Sensory awareness	Music Movement education/ dance Relaxation training How to study Yoga
Personal Relationships	Getting along with others	Friendship training Transactional analysis
Imagery - Interests	Developing self-worth Awareness of imagery Meditation	IALAC story Guided fantasy Imagery training Transcendental meditation
Need to Know	Decision making Identifying irrational ideas	Practice Rational behavior therapy
Guidance of A, B, C's	Attention-paying Assertiveness	Game-playing Behavior rehearsal

Health

Man is a biochemical being, and more emphasis is being placed on the kinds and quality of the food (i.e., diet) that we put in our bodies. This category differs somewhat from the others, but it is nevertheless very important. Although the "basic four" food groups are a start, children need to learn more complete information on nutrition. Fredericks (1964, 1976) provides a comprehensive outline of nutritional needs and their effects on the individual, although the material would need to be simplified for use with different age levels. Some of this input can, of course, be through direct conversation with the child. At other levels, however, the intervention would need to be with the parents (see Chapter 8) or through the school (see Chapter 10).

Emotions-Feelings

The development of awareness and appropriate expression of feelings is best taught in relationship enhancement programs. Certainly a child needs to know how to recognize his/her feelings and to deal with them adequately. This process involves learning how to identify and "own" feelings as well as being able to express them appropriately.

Guerney (1977) and others have developed a model of relationship enhancement that has as one of its basic purposes improved communication through awareness and expression of feelings. These skills are taught systematically, and have been applied to a wide variety of relationships. The Filial Relationship Enhancement program is designed for children under 10 years of age. The technique involves training parents to play with their children at home for prescribed periods of time and in a prescribed way, and also to do this under supervision while they learn the skills. Andronico and Guerney (1967) suggest that Filial Relationship Enhancement programs can be implemented within the school setting so that both teachers and parents could be trained in using these skills with children.

The Parent-Adolescent Relationship Enhancement program is intended for children over the age of 10, and involves a group format where several parents and adolescents learn and practice these skills with the help of trained leaders. Although the use of such programs at present is somewhat limited, Guerney (1977) gives a thorough description of the methods of teaching the skills in these and other related programs. This explicitness provides the reader with the information necessary to implement Relationship Enhancement programs.

The experiencing of joy is definitely a worthy goal and one which many individuals pursue. Schutz (1967) describes a variety of techniques which were intended for adult use, but can be adapted for use in teaching children to experience life more vitally. Singing is frequently seen as a spontaneous outlet for feelings, and Schutz suggests that humming is an enjoyable and simple method for uncovering feelings. For example, a counselor or teacher might ask a child to hum whatever tune came into his/her mind and then discuss the feelings involved in the song. Or perhaps more creative children could hum a tune of their own, making it up as they went along, and then talk about how they felt.

Learning-Sensory (School)

The skill of music involves the child's ability to attend to and appreciate different auditory stimuli. Encouraging children to listen to music is an effective method of developing their auditory skills. This might involve such things as choosing favorite records and identifying particular sounds that they like and/or dislike, and recognizing similar sounds in different records. Or the child might be asked to be very quiet for a short period of time and see how many different sounds he/she can identify.

Motor coordination includes both fine and gross motor skills. Increased practice in these skills can be gained through model-building (Keat, 1974a), catching a ball, and playing jacks. Movement education in the form of movement to basic rhythms and expressive dancing can be useful in developing gross motor coordination as well as auditory appreciation. Valett (1967) describes a number of gross motor activities that can be adapted to different age groups. Increased practice in coordination and expression can also increase feelings of self-worth.

The ability to relax in otherwise stress-producing situations is a skill that a child can develop and use throughout his/her life. Relaxation training can be developed in a variety of ways, as described by Keat (1974b). Especially with young children, the breathing component can be introduced as being helpful, both in relaxation and various sports activities. Deep diaphragm breathing can be practiced by instructing the child to inhale deeply and then to pronounce a syllable such as "s" as he slowly exhales (Keat, 1977). See Appendix A for detailed instructions.

Cue relaxation (Russel & Sipich, 1974) can also be used, particularly with older children. After learning a series of relaxation exercises, the child practices associating a word such as "calm" or "peaceful" with his/her relaxed condition. After repeated pairing of the relaxed feeling with the cue word, the word itself can be used to cue a relaxed response in anxiety-producing situations.

Certainly one of the most basic skills called upon in school settings is the ability to study. This kind of training will help the child to use his/her study time efficiently. Too often it is assumed that the children have these skills when in fact they do not. Training should include such things as how to take notes, time management, how to review for a test, and techniques in memorization.

Zifferblatt (1970) has developed a complete method of study designed for parents to help manage a child's study behavior. He discusses reinforcement techniques, setting up realistic study schedules, and observing behavior. Along similar lines, Chase and Whitbread (1974) explain to parents methods for helping their children in school and how to help the teacher help their child. For the older child, many commercial companies have pamphlets and filmstrips on improving study skills.

Although there are other applications, yoga can be viewed as a method of learning to become aware of bodily sensations and feelings. Yoga classes are offered to adolescents in many communities. Even when these are not available, books such as Hittelman's (1969) provide basic information on beginning and intermediate exercises along with detailed instructions and pictures. Thus, older children would be able to learn some of these skills on their own.

Personal Relationships

As with all of the other modalities, difficulties in interpersonal relationships will affect many other aspects of the child's life. There are relationship skills which the child needs to have in his behavior repertoire. Commercial materials dealing with making friends are available for all age levels. Other programs, such as those described under "Emotions-Feelings" (Guerney, 1977), focus primarily on communication skills. The teacher, therapist-counselor, or parent can also help to develop these skills through discussion and their own modeling behaviors. Bibliotherapy can be used to develop these skills, and Keat, Anderson, Conklin, Elias, and their colleagues (1972) give a list of books available at different reading levels and in different areas. Working with groups of children also lends itself to dealing with interpersonal relationships and resolving conflicts between members.

Transactional analysis has been formulated into several levels of comprehension so that children can better understand interpersonal transactions. TA for Tots (Freed, 1973) is intended for use with elementary age children and helps them to understand their own behaviors and interactions with others. These principles can be taught to children individually or in groups.

Imagery-Interests

The child's feelings of self-worth affect many aspects of his/her development. Simon (1973) has developed a concept and story that is especially useful with helping children to understand their feelings of self and others as well. Based on the idea that everyone needs to feel lovable and capable, the story describes the day of a 14-year-old boy as he goes through a day's "ups" and "downs." Each person can be thought of as wearing an IALAC button (I Am Loveable and Capable) and many of the things we do reflect these needs. Simon points out that put-downs are often efforts to rip off part of someone else's IALAC button to patch on to ours. This story can be read and discussed with chidren, and each child can make a button to dramatize the concepts.

A child can learn to develop imagery skills through many techniques. One might be to have him/her close his/her eyes and imagine a variety of situations, such as being on a beautiful snowy mountain or digging his/her toes into the sand at a beach. A more structured approach might be to "guide" the fantasy through a series of events and then discuss his/her feelings during the incidents.

Lange and Jakubowski (1976) describe the use of a technique called emotive imagery to reduce anxiety to the point where cognitive and behavioral skills can be used. The individual is asked to imagine a scene which engenders good feelings and to get in touch as fully as possible with those feelings. He/she is then to imagine a situation where he/she would like to be more assertive and use positive emotive fantasy to reduce any anxiety. This would seem to be an applicable approach to developing imagery skills in children and adolescents as well.

Transcendental meditation has been gaining in popularity and is generally available to children over the age of four. Several books are now on the market which describe this technique. Robbins and Fisher (1972) cover the method of how to meditate as well as how it works and what it is. Bloomfield, et al. (1975) discuss it in even more detail including physiological data.

LeShan (1974) explores many different types of meditation. For example, he describes a method of "meditation of contemplation." The individual is to focus on a particular object with his/her eyes, studying it carefully for a length of time, and then contrast it with feeling the object.

Need to Know

Beginning in childhood and extending and expanding through his/her adult life, a child will be called on to make decisions. Too often decision making is left to chance and not recognized as the important skill that it is. Although initially the choices are comparatively simple, the process is basically the same as that of dealing with complex situations. Through repeated practice, the children can learn to identify alternatives, explore the consequences of these alternatives and on the basis of this information and their values, make a decision. Values exploration is an important part of this process. In both the home and school settings the child should be given many opportunities to practice these skills. Within the counseling situation, even the young child can be given choices as to activities or games.

Children can be helped to understand the nature of their thoughts about their problems. Ellis and Harper (1975) suggest that after an event at point A, it is the thoughts or things that a person tells himself at point B that cause a reaction at point C. By learning to be aware of this process, children can learn to change "internalized sentences" at point B. After exploring their own thinking patterns, children can learn to modify inappropriate thoughts so that they are more productive and "realistic." This skill would seem to be best suited for older children (ages 9-10 on up), although irrational "self-talk" can be pointed out at almost any age.

Guidance of A, B, C's

The ability to attend to a particular task for a length of time is necessary in many everyday situations, but is probably most heavily called upon in the school setting. Difficulty with this skill will affect many areas and is most frequently seen in young children, although it is by no means limited to that age group.

Game playing is one technique that can be used to increase a child's attention span. Children usually enjoy game playing, especially if it is one they particularly like or have chosen themselves. Initially the games should not be too lengthy. This activity gives the child an opportunity to practice attending to one task; as his/her skill increases, the length of the game can be increased.

Game playing can also be used as a reinforcement for attending to a particular task. For example, the child can be rewarded for completion of a task by playing his/her favorite game, thus giving additional practice in paying attention.

As delineated by Lazarus (1971), assertive behavior refers to one facet of "emotional freedom," and that is to be able to stand up for one's rights. This ability includes such things as the child's ability to question a teacher's directions when he/she hasn't understood them or to be able to express to peers something he/she wishes to do. The ability to express desires is an important aspect of interpersonal relationships and a basic element in any child's behavior repertoire. It is, of course, necessary that this be done in an appropriate manner - in a way that will maximize the probability of the child's expressions being received positively.

Behavior rehearsal is frequently used to expand a child's behavior repertoire. This technique involves both role playing and role reversal, and has been discussed in some detail elsewhere (Keat, 1974a; Krumboltz & Thoresen, 1969). After identifying specific behavior areas, in this case assertive behavior, various alternative responses are explored. The counselor or teacher begins by role playing and modeling possible approaches and responses that the child could use. The roles are then reversed and the child proceeds to practice the assertive behaviors with reinforcement from the counselor.

Keat (1974a) presents a situation in which the child is reluctant to ask his father to help him with a model. In this example the problem area and the child's approach to the situation have already been explored, and the counselor is modeling alternative responses.

Counselor:	O.K. Charlie. It seems that you have some difficulty approaching your father. Let's try something else awhile. Let me be you and you act as you think your father would. O.K.?
Charlie:	Maybe (long pause). I guess I can do it.
Counselor:	All right, let's try it: Hi, Dad. How're you doing?
Charlie:	(Father) Rotten. Can't you see that I'm busy?
Counselor:	Yes, you really seem to have a lot of work to do.
Charlie:	Yeah. Go away and leave me alone.
Counselor:	All right. But can I check with you again in a little while to see if you can help me with my model? I'm stuck now and sure could use your help.
Charlie:	O.K. In a little while.

This is what the child expects to happen. Charlie thinks that his father will reject his advances outright. But, since he expects the worst, almost any outcome is better than anticipating failure and not trying. In this situation, the counselor as Charlie has at least managed a hopeful call-back closure that leaves the door open for future approaches. It would now be appropriate to reverse roles, so that Charlie can play himself using the counselor's model responses.

The counselor's next task is to attempt to anticipate most of the possible responses the child might have to use. The father's responses could range from the anticipated rejection, to saying "Not now, but later," to answering positively.

Counselor:	O.K. Now you be yourself again and I'll be your father.
Charlie:	(After several sessions of rehearsal) Hi, Dad. How's it going?
Counselor:	Pretty bad. How are things with you?
Charlie:	All right. But right now I'm stuck on my model. Could you help me with it sometime?
Counselor:	Sure. Why not now. I'm at a good stopping point.

"Nothing ventured, nothing gained." The child who does not ask for what he wants is unfortunate. By using assertive training combined with behavior rehearsal, the counselor can help the withdrawn child to emerge from his shell. In this procedure an attempt is made to anticipate the major possible reactions to the child's request, have him practice what the counselor models, and reverse roles, thereby developing a repertoire of responses that can enable him to cope better with any eventuality (Keat, 1974a, pp. 72-73).

SUMMARY

There are a variety of activities outlined in the preceding sections that can be used to develop coping and growth skills in children. Any of these activities can be adapted to meet an individual child's interests and needs.

In pursuing our own growth as adults and in HELPING our children, the multimodal approach provides a flexible model in which to work. By using the HELPING acronym, we can utilize a more comprehensive approach toward our children's growth as well as our own.

3 Multimodal Assessment of Individuals

The accurate delineation of problems (concerns, troubles, and so forth) is the necessary first step in an effective treatment program. This multimodal model can provide a chart for differential evaluation, which can help the therapist in choosing a suitable course of action.

An excellent chapter on multimodal assessment was presented by Arnold Lazarus (1976, Chapter 4, pp. 25-47). The purpose herein is only to review this perspective briefly and then to present a series of assessment tables that can help to fill in the evaluation gaps.

"The multimodal assessment process begins with the initial interview" (Lazarus, 1976, p. 25). With regard to inquiry in each modality, Lazarus (1976) presents seven key types of questions for the multimodal therapist to answer. These are (Lazarus, 1976, pp. 30-31):

1. Which particular behaviors do you wish to increase and which ones do you want to decrease?

2. What negative feelings would you like to reduce or eliminate, and what positive feelings would you like to increase or amplify?

3. Among your five senses, what particular reactions would you care to get rid of and what kinds of sensations would you like to magnify?

4. What "mental pictures" or images are bothersome to you so that you would like to erase them, and what pleasant images would you care to bring into clearer focus?

5. Which thoughts, values, attitudes, or beliefs get in the way of your happiness?

6. In your dealings with other people, what gets in the way of close, personal, loving, and mutually satisfying interactions?

7.   Under what conditions do you use drugs (including alcohol, coffee, and tobacco)?

The therapist can use such questions as these (and others) in multimodal inquiry during the course of an interview. The approach should be a flexible one which follows the client's lead for awhile but then goes back to particular avoided or only partially covered zones.

The following tables are presented as a reference base for child assessment if the therapist wants to investigate certain modes in more depth and perhaps in a more objective way. For each cited problem area and related assessment procedure, the test author(s) and/or reference source (with pages) is cited so that you can trace the instrument and use it if you so desire. These procedures, used in a "precision testing" (Keat, 1974a) way, can be utilized for providing diagnostic grist for the multimodal treatment mill.

Table 3-1
Multimodal Assessment: Behavior

Problem, Concern	Assessment (Source)
Assertiveness	Assertiveness Schedule (Lazarus, 1971, pp. 132-133; Rathus, in Thomas, 1974, pp. 258-259)
Behavioral Disorders	Reinforcement Surveys (Keat, 1974a, Appendix D, and Chapter 4 in this book; Clement & Richard in Mash & Terdal, 1976, pp. 207-216)
	Behavioral Checklists (Werry & Quay, 1969; Miller, 1967)
	Formats (Keat, 1974a, pp. 23-28; Kanfer & Saslow, 1969)
Resistance to Counseling	Inner Circle Strategy (Keat, 1974a, pp. 45-46, Lazarus 1971, 81-87)

Table 3-2
Multimodal Assessment: Affect

Problem, Concern	Assessment (Source)
Anxiety, Fear	Fear Survey Schedule (Wolpe & Lang, 1969; Geer in Mash & Terdal, 1976, pp. 155-166)
Social Anxiety	S A D Scale (Watson & Friend, in Mash & Terdal, 1976, pp. 167-183)
General Feelings	Projective Questions (Keat, 1974a, pp. 26-27)

Table 3-3
Multimodal Assessment: Sensations-School

Problem, Concern	Assessment (Source)
Classroom Feelings	Guidance Learning Rating Scale (Keat, 1974a, Appendix F)
Classroom Climate	Classroom Ecology Scale (Chapter 9 of this book)
	Barclay Classroom Climate Inventory (Barclay, 1972)
Fine Perceptual Motor Coordination Tests:	Bender (1938; 1946; & Koppitz, 1964)
	Benton (1963)
	Visual Perception (Frostig, Lefever, & Whittlesey, 1966)
	Gesell Copy Forms (Ilg & Ames, 1964)
	Goodenough-Harris Draw-A-Man Test (Harris, 1963)
Gross Motor Coordination	Purdue Perceptual Motor Survey (Roach & Kephart, 1966)
Psycholinguistic	ITPA (Kirk, McCarthy, & Kirk, 1968)
Speech and Hearing	Riley Articulation and Language Test (Riley, 1966)
Reading	Gray Oral Rading Test (Gray, 1963)

Table 3-4
Multimodal Assessment: Imagery-Interests

Problem, Concern	Assessment (Source)
Interests	Kuder Interest Inventory (Kuder, 1971)
	What I Like to Do (Bonsall, Meyers, & Thorpe, 1958)
Perceptions of Parents	Eidetic Parent's Test (Ahsen, 1972; Ahsen & Lazarus, 1972)
Personal Responses	Thematic Tests (e.g., CAT-H) (Bellack, Bellack, & Hurvich, 1965)
Persons, Things	Sentence Completion (Forer, 1957; Keat, 1974a, p. 123)
Self-concept	Coopersmith (1967) Piers & Harris (1969)

Table 3-5
Multimodal Assessment: Cognition

Problem, Concern	Assessment (Source)
Achievement	Wide Range Achievement Test (Jastak & Jastak, 1965; also the major tests such as California, Iowa, Metropolitan, Stanford)
Aptitudes	Differential Aptitude Test (Bennett, Seashore, & Wesman, 1972)
	General Aptitude Test Battery (GATB, U.S. Employment Service)
Intelligence	Binet (Terman & Merrill, 1960)
	WISC-R (Wechsler, 1974)
	Slosson (Slosson, 1963)
	PPVT (Dunn, 1965)

Irrational beliefs   Survey
                                        (Knaus, 1974, pp. 87-93)

Table 3-6
Multimodal Assessment: Interpersonal Relations

Problem, Concern   Assessment (Source)

Family Interactions   Verbal Problem Checklist
                                        (Thomas, Walter, & O'Flaherty
                                        in Thomas, 1974, pp. 245-256)

                                        Lifestyle Inventory
                                        (Mosak & Shulman, 1971)

Parent Child Interaction   Response-Class Matrix
                                        (Mash, Terdal, & Anderson
                                        in Mash & Terdal, 1976, pp.
                                        305-307)

Marriage Relationship   Marriage Inventory
                                        (Knox, 1971, pp. 138-144)

Social Development   Preschool Attainment Record
                                        (Doll, 1966)

                                        Vineland Social Maturity Scale
                                        (Doll, 1953)

Table 3-7
Multimodal Assessment: Drugs-Diet

Problem, Concern   Assessment (Source)

Alcoholism   Drinking Profile
                                        (Martlatt in Mash & Terdal,
                                        1976, pp. 121-137)

Biochemical Balance   Psychochemical Type
                                        (Watson, 1972, 93-100)

Diet   Dietary Monitoring (Diary) and
                                        History
                                        (Robinson, 1972, pp. 390-393)

4 Turning Children On: A Reward Survey

One of the most important things to determine in working with children is what turns them on - that is, what types of activities and kinds of things are rewarding for them. If we can develop a systematic way of determining what they like, we are then on the royal road to motivating them. Hopefully, of course, some of the tasks they are confronted with in school are reinforcing in and of themselves. The child might enjoy reading and science (in addition to lunch and recess).

But for many of the children we are called upon to help, there is little in the educational system for which they receive warm fuzzies (Freed, 1973). Therefore, one of our tasks as their therapist is to figure out just what might get them turned on so that school might be a more rewarding experience as well as provide cues for parents to use in establishing reinforcement programs.

The search for effective reinforcers is crucial in the practice of therapy with children. Some years ago Cautela and Kastenbaum (1967) presented a reinforcement survey schedule (RSS) for use with adults. While that schedule has some relevant items for children, for the most part it needed to be adapted developmentally (both items and response format). Therefore, as suggested by Cautela and Kastenbaum (1967) that "perhaps a separate RSS will be needed to assess this range and quality of reinforcers to children" (p. 1127), this writer set about developing an appropriate scale to survey possible rewards for elementary school children (Keat, 1974a, Appendix D). A second revision entitled A Survey Schedule of Rewards for Children incorporated some additional items, some deletions, and a changed response set from the first edition (Keat, 1974b).

The reward survey to be presented herein represents the third revision based upon five years of experience using the survey. In addition, the concept of multimodalities (Keat, 1976a; 1976b) has led to a significant restructuring of the survey. In this comprehensive multimodal approach, the therapist systematically assesses seven interactive modes which form the basis of a child's personal life. The different acronym used herein is an adaptation from

31

Lazarus' (1976) BASIC ID modes. The same seven modes are utilized but rearranged to spell HELPING (Keat,1976c; also, see Table 1-3 in Chapter 1 of this volume). In the process of HELPING a child the therapist is concerned about his/her Health (diet), Emotions (feelings), Learnings in life (school-related topics), Personal relationships, Image (self) and Interests, Need to know (cognitive area), and Guidance of acts, behaviors, and consequences. By being aware of the child's functioning in each of these seven areas, the therapist is on the way to effectively HELPING the child.

A REWARD SURVEY

The Reward Survey for Children (RSC) is divided into two sections (see Table 4-1). In the first and largest section (123 items, plus 9 "other" categories), the child responds to a series of items relating to health (diet), life learnings, personal relationships, interests, school activities, and a variety of behaviors. The original response format (Keat, 1974a) was on a four-point scale. For certain children, a more appropriate response set would be on a three-point scale (Keat, 1974b) as used in this article. The simplified three-response format seems to be better for the primary grade child (ages 5 to 8 or 9). In clinical practice with this age group, the author found that the four-response set-up was often confusing in the middle categories. Most children aged 5 to 8 seemed to be able to discriminate better when asked to indicate whether they liked something very much, not at all, or somewhere in the middle ("somewhat"). The four-answer response set is generally more suitable for the intermediate grade child (9 or 10 to 12 years). Children aged 9 to 12 seem to be able to use these middle categories to indicate either a more positive ("a fair amount") or more negative ("a little") leaning (Keat, 1974a, Appendix D). This revised RSC can be used, with the appropriate response format, for the two cited age ranges (5 to 9 use three categories, 10 to 15 use the four-response format). The items are arranged according to the HELPING acronym, that is, Health (items 1 to 4), Emotions (joy, items 5, 6), Learnings (7, 8), Personal relationships (9, 10, 11), Interests (12 to 20), Need to know (21), Guidance of behaviors (22 to 24). The final section of the survey is composed of eight items which are basically projective questions relating to Emotions (items 25, 26), Learnings (27), Personal relationships (28, 29), Self-Image (30), and Guidance of behaviors (31, 32).

Table 4-1
Reward Survey for Children

The items in this questionnaire refer to things and experiences that may give you joy, other pleasurable feelings of attraction, or be of interest to you. Check each item in the column that describes how much you like it now. Answer alongside of each item by checking under the heading which shows how you feel, that is, not at all, somewhat ("a little" or a "fair amount") or very much (a lot).

	Not At All	Somewhat	Very Much
1. Foods			
a. Ice cream	_____	_____	_____
b. Candy	_____	_____	_____
c. Fruit	_____	_____	_____
d. Nuts	_____	_____	_____
e. Pie and cake	_____	_____	_____
f. Cookies	_____	_____	_____
g. Sandwiches	_____	_____	_____
h. Gum	_____	_____	_____
i. Popcorn	_____	_____	_____
j. Seeds, e.g., sunflower	_____	_____	_____
k. Other (list favorites)	_____	_____	_____
l. List your three favorite meals	(1)_____	(2)_____	(3)_____
2. Beverages			
a. Water	_____	_____	_____
b. Milk	_____	_____	_____
c. Soda	_____	_____	_____
d. Cocoa	_____	_____	_____
e. Juices	_____	_____	_____
f. Other ( )	_____	_____	_____
3. Sleeping	_____	_____	_____
4. Taking a bath-shower	_____	_____	_____
5. Like to dance			
a. With boys	_____	_____	_____
b. With girls	_____	_____	_____
c. Ballet	_____	_____	_____
d. Square dancing	_____	_____	_____
e. Folk dancing	_____	_____	_____

	Not At All	Somewhat	Very Much
6. Music			
a. Play instrument ( )	_____	_____	_____
b. Listen to records			
1. Classical	_____	_____	_____
2. Jazz	_____	_____	_____
3. Rock	_____	_____	_____
4. Folk	_____	_____	_____
5. Pop	_____	_____	_____
6. Shows	_____	_____	_____
7. Reading			
a. Comic books	_____	_____	_____
b. Sports	_____	_____	_____
c. Newspapers	_____	_____	_____
d. Adventure	_____	_____	_____
e. Famous people	_____	_____	_____
f. Travel	_____	_____	_____
g. Humor	_____	_____	_____
h. Science	_____	_____	_____
8. School			
a. Language Arts (reading, spelling, etc.)	_____	_____	_____
b. Math	_____	_____	_____
c. Science	_____	_____	_____
d. Lunch	_____	_____	_____
e. Music	_____	_____	_____
f. Art	_____	_____	_____
g. Gym	_____	_____	_____
h. Recess	_____	_____	_____
i. Other ( )	_____	_____	_____

	Not At All	Somewhat	Very Much
9. Talking			
a. With a friend	———	———	———
b. With mother	———	———	———
c. With father	———	———	———
d. With brothers, sisters	———	———	———
e. With adults	———	———	———
f. With teachers	———	———	———
g. Into a tape recorder	———	———	———
10. React to old men and women	———	———	———
11. Like watching other people	———	———	———
12. Animals			
a. Dogs	———	———	———
b. Cats	———	———	———
c. Horses	———	———	———
d. Birds	———	———	———
e. Fish	———	———	———
f. Turtles	———	———	———
g. Other ( )	———	———	———
13. Games			
a. Chess	———	———	———
b. Checkers	———	———	———
c. Puzzles	———	———	———
d. Cards	———	———	———
e. Dominoes	———	———	———
f. Tic Tac Toe	———	———	———
g. Ball	———	———	———
h. Marbles	———	———	———
i. Jacks	———	———	———
j. Pick-up Stix	———	———	———
k. Scrabble	———	———	———
l. Sorry	———	———	———
m. Other ( )	———	———	———

	Not At All	Somewhat	Very Much

14. Play
    a. Cut and paste
    b. Clay
    c. Painting
    d. Drawing (crayons)
    e. Tinker toys
    f. With dolls, puppets
    g. Cars
    h. Lego
    i. Other (   )

15. Material objects
    a. Note pads
    b. Pencils
    c. Crayons
    d. Paper
    e. Coloring book
    f. Eraser
    b. Felt pens
    h. Combs
    i. Flowers
    j. Stamps
    k. Coins
    l. Sports cards, e.g., football
    m. Other (   )

16. T.V.
    List Favorite Programs   (1)_____   (2)_____   (3)_____
                                  (4)_____   (5)_____   (6)_____

17. Movies
    List Favorite Movies   (1)_____   (2)_____   (3)_____
                                  (4)_____   (5)_____   (6)_____

	Not At All	Somewhat	Very Much
18. Hiking or walking	_____	_____	_____
19. Camping	_____	_____	_____
20. Peace and quiet	_____	_____	_____
21. Being praised			
a. About appearance	_____	_____	_____
b. About work	_____	_____	_____
c. About strength	_____	_____	_____
d. About athletic ability	_____	_____	_____
e. About your brain	_____	_____	_____
22. Saying prayers	_____	_____	_____
23. Shopping			
a. Clothes	_____	_____	_____
b. Toys	_____	_____	_____
c. Food	_____	_____	_____
d. Sports equipment	_____	_____	_____
e. Records	_____	_____	_____
f. Other ( )	_____	_____	_____
24. Playing sports			
a. Football	_____	_____	_____
b. Baseball	_____	_____	_____
c. Basketball	_____	_____	_____
d. Golf	_____	_____	_____
e. Swimming	_____	_____	_____
f. Pool	_____	_____	_____
g. Running	_____	_____	_____
h. Tennis	_____	_____	_____
i. Boxing	_____	_____	_____
j. Fishing	_____	_____	_____
k. Hunting	_____	_____	_____

	Not At All	Somewhat	Very Much
l. Skiing	_____	_____	_____
m. Soccer	_____	_____	_____
n. Volleyball	_____	_____	_____
o. Wrestling	_____	_____	_____
p. Other ( )	_____	_____	_____

25. List the things you like best of all in life.

26. If you could buy three games that you like, what would they be?

27. What are the three jobs that you like to do most in the classroom?

28. What do you like to do with your friends?

29. What do you like to do with your parents?

30. If you could change something about yourself, what would it be?

31. What is your allowance? Do you have any other ways of making money?

32. What do you like most to do?

USING THE REWARD SURVEY

The reward survey can be given either individually, in small groups or to entire school classrooms. There are certain developmental considerations, nevertheless, which need to be taken into consideration. Experience over the past five years with the schedule indicates the following types of guidelines:

Individual Administration and Therapy

One-to-one administration is indicated with children aged 5 to 8 years or from kindergarten through third grade. If one is seeing the child in individual therapy, of course, the one-to-one situation would be operant. Then one might view the survey as a format for a structured interview. With young children the therapist can read the items and review the response format (verbally) until the child has the response set established. Older children (aged 11 or 12 years), can either work on the schedule during the session or take it home and bring it back (completed) the following week.

The primary function of using the schedule in individual sessions is to obtain a fairly comprehensive inventory (i.e., 123 closed items, 9 "other" categories, and 8 projective questions) of the child's reward system. By using such a survey, rewards can be discovered which the child might not have thought of on his own. There are at least two additional procedures which the therapist can use once the survey is completed. One is to consult with the child and have him rank order the highly preferred items. That is, if he has indicated a strong attraction for money, sports cars, and games, this procedure would force him to make priorities before a particular reward is used in a program. A second procedure is to have the child assign weights to highly preferred items. These weights can have the dual purpose of showing what the child prefers from among strongly attractive items as well as providing a basis for working toward certain goals on a token basis. For example, to obtain a hockey game might take 25 points. These points could be accumulated on a daily basis by completing particular house chores or homework assignments.

The rewards from the schedule can be used during the therapy sessions, at home by the parents, or in school by the teachers. In particular, behavioral contracts relate directly to the use of the schedule (Keat, 1974a) in all three (individual, small group, classroom) settings.

Small Group Administration and Therapy

With a group the size of five to nine, the scale has been successfully completed by children in the age range of 7 to 9 years. One particular difficulty with the item line-up should be noted. The concern has to do with the visual tracking problem in following the items across the page and down the columns. One solution for this has been to slide a blank piece of paper or a ruler down the page as each item is dealt with. The simplified response format should also help to correct this problem with the younger (5 to 8 year) age group.

Small group sessions may be conducted in the schools. During one of the initial contacts, it is useful to survey the reward system of the group. These rewards can then form the basis for both reinforcement contingencies used in the group - e.g., after you sit and talk for 15 minutes, then you can have the treat - as well as what games to engage in as part of the activity portion of the group session.

Classroom Administration and Utilization

The schedule has been successfully administered to fourth- fifth-, and sixth-grade classes. Administration time is approximately one-half hour. It has been helpful to have an aid in the classroom to deal with questions. At the fourth-grade level it is generally procedurally better to read each item out loud (twice) and allow a brief time for the children to respond. Fifth and sixth graders can generally fill out the inventory on their own.

The survey provides a relatively quick way for the teacher to gain some knowledge about the reward system and interests of her children. This knowledge can then be used for classroom endeavors in which certain clusters of activities may be desired or in determining games for recess.   In particular, question 27 has been useful in establishing behavioral contract components with children in the classroom.   For example, if a child on a behavioral contract achieves so many points (which may be acquired both at home and in school), then he might obtain the privilege of wheeling the TV set into the room.   In this fashion, knowledge of the reinforcement system of the child allows one to encourage more acceptable behavior.

SUMMARY

This chapter describes a multimodal survey of rewards designed for use with children aged 5 to 12.   The survey has two main sections: (1) a series of items about health, emotions, learnings in life, personal relationships, interests, need to know (cognition), and a variety of behavioral activities; (2) projective questions of relevance to the child's feelings, classroom jobs, friends and parents, self-image, allowance and their most enjoyable activities in life.

The reward survey can be profitably used individually, with small groups of children, as well as with entire classrooms.   The primary use individually is to either structure a session with younger children (ages 5 to 8) or to obtain a comprehensive catalogue of rewards for the older (ages 9-12) youngster so that you can use various reinforcements constructively both during the sessions as well as making suggestions to the parents for rewarding their child.   Behavioral contracting, based upon a reward survey, is utilizable in all three of the discussed settings.   The Reward Survey for Children can be used to formulate the activities for therapy with small groups of children.   Finally, the RSC can be utilized to obtain the collective reinforcements for an entire classroom which can lead to structuring of school activities as well as establishing contingencies for behavioral contracts for the entire classroom (e.g., work for a party) or individual agreements for children within the class (e.g., accumulate points for extra time in an emotional resource center, Keat, 1974a).

5 Multimodal Counseling With Children: Treating the Basic Id

This is a case for the BASIC ID: A psychoanalytic treatment of a case? No! The BASIC ID has been proposed recently as a multimodal approach to counseling (Lazarus, 1973, 1974a, 1974b, 1976). In this broad spectrum and comprehensive approach each letter of the acronym "BASIC ID" represents a component of a profile to use for both problem identification and the planning of counseling strategies: Behavior, Affect, Sensation (School), Imagery, Cognition, Interpersonal relationships, Drugs - Diet. I have found this multimodal approach to be useful for analyzing, organizing, and integrating case studies both for my own understanding as well as for presentations to parents. It represents a type of "head profile" to guide comprehensive assessment and treatment of one's more difficult cases.

This writer's task has been to develop this model for application to child counseling with elementary school children. Previously, cases of two boys, aged 7 and 9 have been presented via the BASIC ID framework (Keat, 1976a). This article will illustrate the approach by developing the case of a young girl (aged 9).

CASE BACKGROUND

The client, Demaris (aged 9), came from an intact family composed of a father and mother plus two younger sisters. Both parents were well educated. One sister was one year behind Demaris in the same elementary school while the other sister was attending nursery school one-half day. Both younger children had experienced physical (medical) difficulties which had placed great stress on the family system in the past. The major presenting problem identified by the parents for Demaris were encopresis, lying, difficulty with

* From <u>Pennsylvania Personnel and Guidance Association Journal</u>, 1976, <u>4</u>, 21-25. Reprinted by permission.

math in school, low self-image, poor frustration tolerance, and a fear of failure.

After the first session with the parents, the counselor noted that they seemed to be at their wits' end. Each had absorbed so much stress within the family system that Demaris represented the straw that promised to break the camel's back. Mother, especially, was locked in a dyadic struggle with her oldest daughter and a full-blown conflict was in evidence.

The following multimodal case analysis utilizing the BASIC ID approach represents a summary of an initial parent contact, two sessions with Demaris, an interview with the parents and representative school personnel, two more contacts with the identified client (child), and a final counseling session with the parents.

Table 5-1 - "BASIC ID"
Multimodal Profile for Demaris

Mode	Problems	Treatment
Behavior	Encopresis	Behavioral contract
		Restitution
	Lying	Bibliotherapy
Affect	Anger	Directed muscular activity
		Puppet play
		Inhibition training
	Anxiety	Relaxation
		T-F-D games
Sensation-School	Low in math	Remedial work - tutor
	Kinesthetic	Encourage physical things
Imagery	Low self-image	Reinforcement study
		Bibliotherapy
		Self-disclosure
Cognition	Self-putdowns	Corrective self-talk
	Fears failure	Games and bibliotherapy
	Low frustration	
	tolerance	Corrective experiences
Interpersonal relationships	Sibling rivalry	"Instant replay"
	Conflict with mother	Parent counseling
		Self-plans
		Family council
Drugs-Diet	Diet	More controlled food intake
	Supplements	Megavitamin therapy

PROBLEMS AND COUNSELING INTERVENTIONS

Behavior

The primary presenting problem of Demaris was encopresis (i.e. daytime soiling). This behavior was particularly distressing to the parents because she would soil her pants and then hide them somewhere in her room. A few days following the hiding behavior (pants were usually placed in her bureau drawers), the odor in her room would become almost unbearable. The particular intervention in this situation was literally that Demaris become "unshitified" (Ellis, 1973). Inspection of Table 5-1 discloses there were primarily two interventions of direct relevance for this difficulty. It should not be forgotten, however, that due to the interdependence of the modes, therapeutic strategies in one mode can have an influence in another (e.g. treating anger had a direct bearing on the child's main presenting problem, encopresis). The first direct intervention was the establishing of behavioral contracts with Demaris. Procedures were discussed during the initial session with the parents, and they were given Patterson (1971) and Madsen and Madsen (1972) to read. With the counselor's and the books' guidance, these parents developed an intricate series of contracts involving all three children. Despite some initial discouragement because of time involved in the preparation of the contracts (posted on the refrigerator), they did stick with them and after about two months were elated that their child was symptom free. It is felt that behavioral contracting, combined with "restitution" (Keat, 1974a), was the primary reason for success.

The second presenting behavioral concern was that of lying. (Once the primary problem of encopresis was resolved, reasons for lying were diminished). The main intervention strategy was that of bibliotherapy. In this procedure Demaris read relevant stories, e.g., "The $100 Lie" (Gardner, 1972). We would then discuss the story and lessons learned from it. There was a lessening of lying reported by the parents.

Affect

In the affective mode there are two major feelings which typically need treatment with referred children - anger and anxiety. With regard to anger, Demaris was taught various ways to deal with this feeling. On the physical level, directed muscular activities (DMA) were used. This procedure involved teaching her how to direct aggressive feelings in a pre-programmed way into inanimate objects, e.g., pillows. It often enhances the effect of such activities to have the child draw a picture of the hated person on a foam rubber pad designed to be pummeled. On the verbal level, she was encouraged to develop a feeling vocabulary to express how she felt. It is, of course, important that words used be acceptable to persons in the environment (Keat, 1976a). On the imagery level, it was important for

Demaris to know that it was all right to imagine doing things to a disliked person (e.g., "I'd like to punch my mother in the mouth," or "I wish my teacher would drop dead") but as Henny Penny says, "Wishing doesn't make it so." As part of anger inhibition training, children need to learn appropriate modes of expression, what they can do and when they can do it. In a sense, puppet play is a circumscribed area in which children can express their affects. Demaris would go through the family and note realistic interactions between herself (a girl puppet) an various family members. Most of the anger flowed between the girl and mother puppets. Once appropriate channels for anger expression were developed, her need to get back at her mother diminished and thus her soiling behavior diminished.

The second major affect of concern was anxiety. The best antidote for this feeling is usually relaxation training, a procedure which involves training in deep breathing, tension control (isometric exercises), and pleasant imagery development (Keat, 1974b). To enhance the development of relaxation skills, one needs to make them appealing to children (Koeppen, 1974).

Another procedure useful in enhancing the expression of feelings is the Talking, Feeling and Doing game (Gardner, 1973). This technique encourages the child to express important emotions which might otherwise be inhibited (e.g., feelings toward teachers, parents).

Sensation-School

In recent presentations of the BASIC ID method of analysis (Keat, 1976), it occurred that practically every intervention with a child in the sensation area had to do with some school-related skill (e.g., reading, handwriting, perceptual motor deficits, etc.). Therefore, the term "school" can be used interchangeably with "sensation." In the case of Demaris, her particular circumscribed deficiency was in the area of mathematics. Therefore, special remedial help was sought through the use of a tutor. In addition, painstaking care was taken to get her with a teacher who would be good for her. Much of the gain in this case can probably be attributed to getting her a therapeutic teacher for third-grade classes. Likewise, her positive physical (i.e., kinesthetic) skills were encouraged, and she was given lots of "warm fuzzies" (Freed, 1973) for such things as dancing, swimming, and various playground activities.

Imagery

Low self-image is a commonly encountered syndrome in referred children. In order to enhance one's self-concept, there are a variety of strategies which can be considered. First, determine the child's personalized reinforcement contingencies, that is, survey what her needs and reinforcers are (Keat, 1974a). Once these reinforcers are determined, one can reward a child more meaningfully and thus enhance her self-image. Secondly, bibliotherapy can be utilized. Such stories as the "Ugly Duck" (in Gardner, 1974) and Homer the Homely Hound (Garcia & Pellegrini, 1974) can be useful in helping the child learn how to cope with feelings of low self-esteem, fear of failure, and obtaining friends.

Cognition

A basic premise of the rational approach to counseling is that we upset ourselves by our own belief (thought, cognitive) system (Ellis, 1962, 1973; Ellis & Harper, 1975; Young, 1974). Demaris was fearful of failure because of her numerous self-putdowns. Therefore, it was necessary to train her in some corrective self-talk, e.g., "You're really O.K.," "You can do lots of good things," and so forth. In order to enhance the self-sentence reprogramming process, a series of sentences were taped for her listening. In addition, it was also necessary to cue the parents in on this approach. Therefore, two handouts involving 11 rational points of emphasis (Lazarus, 1971) and 10 guidelines for child management (Keat, 1974b, adapted from Hauck, 1972) were given to the parents. The former are mostly to promote the parents' own rational living, while the latter are general principles for parents. It was also deemed necessary that mother curtail her "cold pricklies" (Freed, 1973) directed toward her daughter.

Low frustration tolerance is commonly encountered in children. The counselor can use some games to help the child to learn to deal with this. For example, Demaris tended to feel that she needed to win at a hockey game. As the outcome was tenuously in the balance, sentences were repeated (if repeated enough, hopefully internalized) such as "It would be nice to win, but if you don't, it will still be O.K."

Interpersonal Relationships

Sibling rivalry is to be expected in families. If it is excessive, some intervention strategies should be planned. In Demaris' family she had an intense conflict with the closest (separated only by one year) sister. Bibliotherapy was instituted in order to help with the situation. Instant Replay (Bedford, 1974) was used with Demaris, and the general stop action, communication, rational, and problem-solving approach was explained to the parents. An additional procedure used with the mother and the family was to first direct the mother to get off her daughter's back. Second, to explore ways for the mother to direct her energies and thus drain off her feelings. A "family council" (Dreikurs, Gould, & Corsini, 1974) procedure was instituted for the family. This procedure tends to redistribute conflict areas and helps to ease family tension by allowing the children to have some voice in a democratic fashion.

Drugs-Diet

No medication was involved in this case. With regard to medication, however, it should be noted that the counselor's responsibility is to monitor (with the teacher's help) a medicated child's behavior and report to both parents and physician regarding regulation of appropriate dosage.

With regard to diet, more situational eating controls were implemented (Stuart & Davis, 1972) so Demaris would not ingest so much "junk food." In general, special diets may be useful with hyperactive children (Feingold, 1975). The writer has another client who has recently gone off Ritalin after instituting the "K-P" diet (Feingold, 1975).

SUMMARY

This case presentation has illustrated the application of a multimodal approach to the counseling of the identified client (9-year-old child) and her family. The BASIC ID profile was presented as a systematic approach to problem analysis and proposed intervention strategies. The outcomes from utilization of such a broad spectrum multimodal approach were quite positive. Despite the typical difficulty with such problems (Horne, 1974), the major presenting problems were resolved and positive gains were noted in the various modes after only three parent and four child sessions.

6 Multimodal Therapy
With an Adolescent

The flexibility of the multimodal approach allows the therapist to move from working with adults, to children, to adolescents. What is required is a somewhat different BASIC ID score as one uses the multimodal approach to orchestrate your therapy approach. The previously discussed musical analogy can provide one with analogous approaches. The case of Demaris was presented as a C (child) Minor study, the case of Burt will be presented as an A Minor composition. The adolescent as a minor person moving into adulthood (which will be A Major or A Dominant for the parenting chapter - see Chapter 8).

THE CASE OF BURT

The identified patient in this family was Burt, a 16-year-old adolescent. He was the only child in a family composed of a legally blind and overweight mother (aged 50), a labor-worker father (52 years of age), and a grandmother in her mid-60s who was still working. The family lived in the grandmother's house along with 16 cats.

The case was referred to me by a MH/MR center caseworker and was presented as either being a welfare case or a medical assistance situation. Burt had a history of special education class placements (ED) and there was a thick chart available about him. The two main reasons presented for the referral were that the psychologist felt he needed: (1) vocational counseling and appropriate classroom placement, and (2) that he was psychotic. He was withdrawn, heard and talked to imaginary companions (25 persons lived in his closet, although he also conversed with some historical figures, such as Lincoln, in school). In addition, he talked to plants, and ghosts existed for him. It seemed as though one of my initial goals would be to enable him to function outside of a mental institution.

After several sessions with Burt, problems in various modes emerged (in

47

addition to the just discussed imagery and cognitive ones). These were his strange behaviors (he would jump out of his seat and wander vaguely around the room; at times he would check out dark corners for ghosts; closets could not be opened due to the possible presence of ghosts); mannerisms, tenseness, and inappropriate laughter, rapid and confused speech which was often difficult to understand, shyness and lack of responsibility for personal things (his parents would push up his glasses if they slid down his nose), and he was overweight. The Modality Profile presented in Table 6-1 organizes these presenting problems along with the utilized and ongoing treatment plans which will be discussed in the BASIC ID order.

Table 6-1 - "BASIC ID"
Multimodal Profile for Burt

Modality		Problems	Treatment
Behavior	B1	Strange mannerisms	Confrontation. Retraining, Eye contact, Model
	B2	Rapid-confused speech	Relax, slow down
	B3	Passivity	Model assertive training
Affect	A1	Anxiety	Relaxation, modeling
	A2	Anger (overly repressed)	Encourage expression, Directed muscular activity
	A3	Humor	Discussion of appropriate expression; controls during session
Sensations- School	S1	School difficulties	Teacher conference, Supplemental curriculum
	S2	Reading well	Accentuate skill
Imagery	I1	Fantasy-reality conflict	Debate and point out alternative notions, Books (information-giving) Suggest limiting TV
	I2	Dreams	Discuss and tie to life's realities
Cognitive	C1	Religious dogma	Discussions and reading
	C2	Mistaken ideas and dichotomous reasoning	Rational-emotive
	C3	Sexual curiosity	Bibliotherapy, talk, factual intervention
	C4	Job choice	Career exploration

Modality		Problems	Treatment
Interpersonal Relations	IP1	Problems with peers (shy)	Friendship training, Bibliotherapy
	IP2	Personal relationships	T.A. reading and training
	IP3	Kind, considerate	Positive reinforcement
Drugs-Diet	D1	Overweight	Diet therapy/weight control; exercise program
	D2	Nutritional deficiencies	Megavitamin therapy

PROBLEMS AND TREATMENT STRATEGIES

Behavior

At my first meeting with Burt, I was taken by his variety of strange mannerisms. He looked and acted differently. During our initial sessions he could only sit still for a brief period of time and then he would jump out of his seat and wander around the office. Sometimes this was random (ghost-searching) or specific (girl watching out the window). In order to deal with this in vivo, I would initially stay in my seat to model more appropriate behavior. If he did not soon return, sometimes I would join him in either the girl watching or ghost chasing (I would open the dark closet door and whisk away the ghosts). As far as staying-in-seat behaviors, Burt was retrained to have appropriate eye contact, hand movements, and I would gently confront him regarding his inappropriate behaviors.

Another difficulty was Burt's rapid and confused speech patterns. With anyone experiencing this difficulty the problem can be compounded by constantly being asked to repeat what has just been said. Therefore, I would concentrate on his relaxing and slowing down (sometimes with hand signals) so that he could be understood. At times, of course, repeating would be necessary, but by having him learn to slow down, much of his incoherence was cleared up.

Another major behavior problem was his general passivity in almost any situation. Although passivity can help keep things peaceful, Burt would occasionally have his personal rights violated. Therefore, these situations were discussed with him. More assertive responses were presented and behavioral rehearsal was implemented in order to help him learn more appropriate ways of standing up for his rights.

Affect

Anxiety seemed to be an overwhelming burden for Burt and probably triggered some of his out-of-seat behavior. Three main antidotes were utilized here. The first procedure was relaxation training via bibliotherapy and tapes. Burt rejected the children's tapes because of the eerie background music. He also resisted other tapes on relaxation and therefore we resorted to in-session personalized practice. The second procedure was to use bibliotherapy. Burt again resisted these materials but his father did read and implement (for himself and his son) some of the ideas from Jacobson (1962). Finally, the most useful procedure with Burt was my role as a calm and serene model. This effect was verbalized by "whenever I see you I feel much cooler and calmer."

As in most cases, the second main affect of concern was anger expression. The difference here, however, was that Burt was typically overly repressed. He seemed to believe that any expression of anger was negative. Therefore, my task was first to undo some of this belief system and to encourage constructive outlets for his angry feelings. One of these outlets was directed muscular activity (DMA) whenever he felt frustrated or angry about something. Since he is such a "bottled-up" person, he needed constant encouragement in order to show such emotions.

While humor is a necessary ingredient in happy living, the excessive use of laughter can become bizarre. Burt would occasionally become locked into a laughter cycle which could be difficult to break into. The curtailment would initially involve getting him to simmer down, then discuss what set him off, talk about the appropriate use of laughter and work on controlling it during our session. Generalization of controls is also important because laughing out loud inappropriately (e.g., during a family-school conference) can be damaging to the adolescent's image in the eyes of others.

Sensations - School

As was mentioned, Burt was placed in a special class for emotionally disturbed (ED) children. Herein lies another beauty of the multimodal system. Although much of this case analysis focuses on the individual, in the school and interpersonal zones we will freely intervene in the other major life environments of the child (school and home).

In the school arena, periodic conferences help to keep both teacher and therapist in touch. The therapist can aid by making suggestions for the classroom and talking about books which can be used as supplemental curriculum.

Many adolescents will accept required reading from their teachers better than they will from their therapist. One of Burt's strengths was that he could read (visual mode) quite well. But he preferred science fiction, mysteries, and ghost stories to non fiction. Therefore, direct suggestions were made for the teacher to require that he read for in-class discussion. Books like You (Gordon & Conant, 1975) and Born to Win (James & Jongeward, 1971) are illustrations of books utilized in this way. I will cite several other coordinated (between teacher and therapist) readings under the cognitive and interpersonal relations modes.

Imagery

Although the modes are presented in the BASIC ID order, as previously mentioned in Chapter 1, the therapist may want to start in one mode and then shift gears into other zones. The Behavior mode is usually the first area of intervention when working with children. With adults the most elegant solutions are usually in the Cognitive zone. Due to the nature of this adolescent's disturbance, the Imagery mode was felt to be the most important zone for the initial focus. This was due to his auditory and visual hallucinations, the existence of ghosts, and in general, a difficulty in deciphering what was real and what was imaginary, (or in his "minds-eye".)

An example of one of his beliefs was that the star of The Six Million Dollar Man, Steve Austin, could really do all of the superman feats they showed on television. Burt believed that his bionics were real and that he could actually jump 20 feet in the air, run 60 miles an hour, zoom in with his bionic eye, and lift cars. At times he would even try some of these superman feats in the office by attempting to lift a heavy (loaded down with books) table. Initial discussion of how they might be tricking the viewer was relatively ineffective. He still clung to his beliefs. Therefore, we drafted a letter to the associate producer of the television show. Part of the associate producer's answer is the following:

> Now, as to the most important question that you ask - Is Steve Austin real? The answer, gentlemen, is no.
> You see, Steve Austin was made up from a writer's mind. He got an idea and then wrote his idea on paper. The studio liked his idea and transferred it into a T. V. series. Now - since Steve Austin is nothing more than a role that Lee Majors portrays he cannot lift any more than the average man. Sure it appears that Steve can run and lift things with fantastic speed and strength, but this is done with a trick camera. As a matter of fact, almost any stunt performed on the show is done this way. I'm sorry that Steve Austin isn't a real person, but the star, Lee Majors is, and he told me to tell you two guys hello."
> There was also a P.S.: "Your teacher and therapist are nice people, and you can trust them."

After this, we would usually spend the session after the Sunday night show discussing the tricks Steve performed and how they might have set them up to trick us. Great inroads were made into his imaginary belief system. It also illustrates the importance of the child therapist being aware of and tuned into the client's world. It is often necessary to watch relevant T. V. shows and do other things (play games) which adult therapists typically would not do.

Much of Burt's imaginary life was related to his T. V. viewing and science fiction reading. Regarding the initial stimulus (T.V.), I discussed with his parents the limiting of some of his T. V. watching (e.g., Nightstalker). They could do this both by selecting some of their own reality-based shows as well as encouraging him to get into some other activity around the house.

Burt's dreams were usually related to me in a laughing manner. "How ridiculous and silly they are. I can't imagine what they're about." Quite often they involved his school teacher. These dreams were content analyzed and related to his real life situation. In all of our discussions about fantasy-reality events, I constantly tried to keep our feet firmly planted in the land of reality. Progress in this zone has been slow but constant.

Cognition

An area related to the imagery system of Burt was his religious ideology dogma. The family was very tied into religious beliefs and he reflected their investment. Although this relates to some of his beliefs in imaginary things, the part that was more bothersome was that he felt he would be taken care of by God and that the control of his life was out of his hands - that whatever happened was willed externally. Therefore, it was necessary to attempt to work from within his ideological base (to contradict the system would have alienated the family) and try to reprogram him with other sayings like "God helps those that help themselves," that is, to "Be the best of what you can be" in order to shift responsibility for behaving back on Burt. A source that proved to be useful in reinterpreting the Bible's messages which Burt was using was Good News for Modern Man (Bratcher, 1971) which presents the New Testament in today's English.

The major procedure utilized in this mode was the rational one of dealing with his mistaken ideas. For example, mistaken idea #4 states that "You are a victim of circumstances. Your life is basically controlled by outside forces" (Lazarus & Fay, 1975, p. 42). Therefore, we challenged his external locus of control ideas, wrote down more realistic ones, and repeated them periodically so that the new self-sentences might become internalized. In order to further acquaint him with this viewpoint, he read Young (1974), which combines the rational viewpoint with interesting illustrative drawings. These types of books with pictures are often more enticing for adolescents.

This statement is especially true in the area of sex education. Several sources were used with Burt and included The Miracle of Sex (Boria, 1970), What's Happening to Me (Mayle, Robins, & Walter, 1975), Boys and Sex (Pomeroy, 1968). These sources were read and discussed together during the therapy hours.

The final area of consideration in this mode was to explore possible job choices. Burt would come up with some unrealistic choices such as actor, writer (poet), or radio announcer. It was necessary to discourage these types of choices due to his speech difficulties (actor and radio announcer) and have him try to write something for me (which he never did). It was important not to be too discouraging, but to encourage him to consider more realistic alternatives. Some of these included referral to the Bureau of Vocational Rehabilitation (BVR) for evaluation and possible placement in a horticulture training program. Plants were an interest of Burt's and it was felt that he could handle the training and eventual job placement. Another possibility explored was food service in a restaurant. These alternatives will continue to be explored and developed as he enters the final few months of his public school program. This is an extremely crucial consideration as we attempt to move him toward a responsible place in society.

Interpersonal Relations

Burt spent most of his time outside of school with the adults (mother, father, grandmother) in his house. His relationships with adults were, therefore, typically quite adequate and appropriate. The task with his parents was to encourage them to let him go more on his own and to seek out additional peer interaction. We discussed these "letting-go" strategies during family sessions. They included such things as encouraging him to go out of the house and play ball (added benefit of exercise) at his own basket, to move across the street to play on the public playground, and call other adolescents and invite them over or go to their houses.

As can be gleaned from the above, most of his interpersonal problems were with peers. It was not that he didn't get along. He was passively shy and relatively uninvolved with them (somewhat like an observer). Therefore, we initiated friendship training (Keat & Guerney, 1978). This procedure involves a series of three steps in which you train the individual to meet, greet, and then keep friends. In the meeting stage, we discussed ways in which he could put himself in situations in which he could meet other adolescents (e.g., school, church, playground). Then we rehearsed various ways in which he could greet the other persons (e.g., Hi. How are you? What do you feel like doing today?). Finally (and this is probably the most difficult and all encompassing stage), we discussed ways to keep friends. This step essentially involves moving yourself toward being an interesting and likable person. In order to be interesting, you need to have a variety of interests and skills in doing things like reading and games. To be likable, you need to be able to listen to others, share things with them, and show that you care for them in some way. Burt was trained to meet, greet, and keep a few friends, but he still generally preferred to spend the bulk of his time with his family, reading, or watching T. V. Some of the useful bibliotherapeutic sources read during sessions included pamphlets from the American Guidance Service Coping Series (e.g., Schwarzrock & Wrenn, 1973; Wrenn & Schwarzrock, 1970). Other bibliotherapeutic sources which were read during sessions, at school and/or at home included You (Gordon & Conant, 1975), TA for Teens (Freed, 1976), Born to Win (James & Jongeward, 1971), and a whole series of books relating to transactional analysis (TA), for example, Bry, (1973, 1975, 1976). TA is a relatively simple method of understanding interpersonal exchanges and Burt was able to read the books, grasp the concepts, and with a little help apply some of the games to his own life interactions. These applications included both home and school. He became the classroom expert on TA.

With regard to Burt's other positive interpersonal characteristics, he was both kind and considerate. These characteristics were given continual support and positive reinforcement in order to maintain these good characteristics at a high level of occurrence.

Drugs - Diet

Burt evidenced both overweight and some skin blemishes. It was expected that dietary interventions would be helpful with these problems. The general paradigm followed was that of Stuart and Davis (1972), which is a three-component program. With regard to caloric intake, I initiated discussions with the family. The mother also tended to be very heavy and therefore the food source provider proved to be difficult to change. But we did go over particular food groups, the value of natural foods, things (e.g., salt and sugar) to avoid, and so forth. The situational components were covered and parents were asked to monitor and curtail goodies ingested during T.V. time. Finally, I checked with Burt on a weekly basis as to just what he had done regarding exercise. This check involved both home and school situations. Burt's weight slowly decreased. This decrease was aided by a week-long illness during which he essentially fasted (Cott, 1975).

Due to the nature of his nutritional deficiencies, it was felt that a megavitamin regime might be helpful to attain a biochemical balance in his body. In turn, I hoped that such a balancing could also have benefit across other modalities and positively effect his behaviors and images. Therefore, in order to initiate a megavitamin therapy program, the outline presented in Table 6-2 was given to the parents. This program was derived from such sources as Rimland (1968) and Cott (1974).

Table 6-2
Megavitamin Therapy Program

Dear Parents:

After considering a large quantity of individual case history material and published reports, the following regime is suggested as a point of departure for your child's vitamin therapy.

Days 1-14 (2 weeks)

1. Vitamin C (free of lactose base). One gram daily per 50 lbs. body weight.

2. B Complex Vitamin, with the following guidelines for choosing it:

Choline	50 mg.
Inositol	50 mg.
Folic acid	100 mcg.
Pantothenic acid	50 mg.

Para-aminobenzoic acid (PABA = 30 mg.)

Biotin	=	15 mcg.
B_1 (Thiamin)	=	5 mg.
B_2 (Riboflavin)	=	5 mg.
B_3 (Niacinamide)	=	30 mg.
B_6 (Pyridoxine)	=	5 mg.
B_{12}	=	10 mcg.

3. Niacinamide (B_3) = One gram daily per 50 lbs. body weight starting at 100 mg. and reaching full dosage over 20 week period.

<u>Days 15-28 (weeks 3 and 4)</u>

4. Child given vitamin B_6 (Pyridoxine). Approximately 15 to 20 mg. per 100 mg. of B_3 (Niacinamide) till full dosage of B_3 is reached.

<u>Days 20-35 (week 5)</u>

5. Continue 1, 2, 3, and 4 above.

<u>Days 36-120 (weeks 6 to 17)</u>

6. Continue 1, 2, 3, and 4. Add 200 mg. pantothenic acid per day.

Summary:

This regime was designed to provide maximum benefit from the ingredients while still introducing vitamins separately, insofar as possible, so that adjustments may be made as needed.

If you have any questions or concerns, please call me.

Donald B. Keat II, Ph.D.
Multimodal Child Psychologist

The results of this program were clouded. Parents were unsystematic in implementing and carrying out the program and after awhile it tailed off with only some vitamins being given (e.g., C, B-complex). Burt's complexion did clear up during this program.

DISCUSSION

This case illustrates the application of multimodal therapy to 19 target areas within the seven zones. Therapeutic gains were noted for most of the intervention problems. Some of the concerns have remained relatively unaltered. But the case is still in treatment and continual efforts will be made to help this adolescent and his family. After all, it can be remembered that just keeping this boy out of a mental hospital and functioning in society can be construed as a major accomplishment.

In order that you might further see the usefulness of the multimodal approach, I will present verbatim letters which were written to the supporting MH/MR Base Service Unit. The first letter was written after six months of treatment. In it the model is briefly explained and the modes are systematically explored.

Table 6-3
Initial Letter to MH/MR Supporting Facility

RE: Burt

Dear Mrs. G:

As per our conversation today, the following letter is the outline of goal statements and a progress report on Burt. It is my judgment that he is in need of further psychotherapy and the purpose of this letter is to support authorization for further services. The psychological report recommended "individual treatment of long duration."

Due to my orientation, I analyze cases from a multimodal viewpoint. What follows is taken from Burt's chart and represents a "BASIC ID" (i.e. B-Behavior, A-Affect, S-Sensations, I-Imagery, C-Cognitions, I-Interpersonal Relationships, D-Drugs-Diet) Approach to psychotherapy. For each letter of the BASIC ID acronym, I will briefly mention diagnostic observations as well as treatment methods.

Behavior(s). Burt exhibits a variety of strange behaviors. During sessions he is confronted when appropriate, and these confrontations are timed properly. He still has numerous mannerisms which I am attempting to modify.

Affect. His outstanding presenting characteristic is his "nervous condition." To combat this, we have used relaxation tapes (which he has resisted) and provided a relaxed model (myself). With regard to this symptom, he claims "you've cured me". He has made some gains, but not to the extent he has stated. Anger is an affect in which he is overly inhibited. To help him to express this emotion, I have encouraged verbal expression of mad feelings as well as used directed muscular activities. An emotion which he can use well is humor. This has been utilized by reading comic books with psychological messages (e.g., Behaviorman, IALAC).

Sensations-School.   One   of   Burt's   difficulties   has   been   eliciting understandable speech. During individual and family sessions he occasionally was instructed to slow down so that he would be understandable. He seems to be internalizing some of this control. With regard to school work, there have been numerous phone conversations and one in-person contact with the teacher. These contacts have been to consult and coordinate efforts. As evidenced by his most recent report card, his work has improved. Reading is his asset and is encouraged.

Imagery. Initially, Burt presented his dreams and these were analyzed. Now we have moved into the core of his pathology, i.e. differentiating between fantasy-reality and his belief in ghosts, etc. Slight inroads have been made on his delusional system but there remains much to be done in this mode.

Cognition.   Burt   tells   himself   numerous   strange   statements.   Wherever possible, I attempt to reprogram his belief system in a more rational sense. In addition, he has expressed an interest in sex. Therefore, we have read numerous books which present sex information in straightforward fashion.

Interpersonal Relationships. Burt gets along well with adults. He has some difficulty, nevertheless, with peers. Some bibliotherapeutic sources have been used for friendship training.

Diet. An attempt has been made to alter Burt's eating habits. After speaking with Burt and his teacher, it was determined that some diet therapy suggestions were in order. Some possible dietary alterations were discussed with the parents. In addition, a megavitamin therapy program has been instituted. The parents have a two page outline, by days, of a regimen to introduce various vitamins in an attempt to balance Burt's biochemical system. We are about one-third into the program.

In summary, psychotherapeutic efforts have been along the broad spectrum of modes just discussed. As noted, there have been some gains in each area, but Burt still has a long way to go. He probably will need long term psychotherapy both to maintain and enhance his functioning.

Sincerely yours,

Donald B. Keat II. Ph.D.
Multimodal Child Psychologist

Table 6-4 illustrates a therapy progress report about one and one-half years after the one shown in Table 6-3. This summary represents the current status of the case.

Table 6-4
Most Recent Letter to MH/MR unit

RE: Burt

Dear Mrs. G:

Burt is still in need of continued psychotherapy. This statement is especially true at this time in his life as he is about to leave the school system and attempt to gain a productive place in society. As I have done in the four previous letters regarding authorization, I will outline his case from a multimodal therapy perspective and will incorporate both goals and gains under each of these seven headings.

Behavior(s). The movement in this mode has been to continue Burt toward assuming more responsible behaviors, that is, to help around the house more, to be more independent in his functioning, to consider options for future roles in the community.

Affect. Burt continues to progress in his contest with undue anxiety. Through the use of discussions and modeling, he seems to be coping better.

School. The major inroad in this zone has been Burt's movement into more nonfiction reading. Although he prefers to read science fiction and mysteries, he has been reading such books as Games People Play and Born to Win. Through such bibliotherapeutic sources, he is gaining helpful knowledge about people and himself. In addition, he now observes things in his classmates which he used to think and do and comments on their strange thoughts and bizarre actions.

Imagery. Burt has made great gains in this area. He can now observe his school classmates and comment on their bizarre fantasies. As he can evaluate their pathologies, he has gained insights into his own distorted fantasies. Also, he now accepts the camera tricks on such shows as his favorite, The Six Million Dollar Man.

Cognitive. Burt is now in 12th grade and will be graduating in June. Within the next two months we need to make a referral to BVR and follow up on this so that he can have some concrete plans to implement during the summer. Many of his vocational plans are unrealistic (e.g., radio announcer, writer, actor). Therefore, part of each session is now being devoted to exploring more realistic options such as plant care, food service, and post office work.

Interpersonal Relationships. Burt's peer relationships are getting to be more age appropriate. As this happens, however, we are being faced with the complications of his becoming more interested in girls on a reality level. We've been discussing dreams, reading sex education books, and discussing men and women as individuals as well as in their relationships.

Diet. Food intake is one of the usual topics for our monthly family sessions. In addition, vitamin supplements are discussed. Grandmother is especially interested in this. She is an important consideration in this family because she is probably the major power in the family.

In summary, Burt continues to make positive progress. He can benefit from continued psychotherapy especially as he is about to confront one of the major crises of his life, that is, the choice of a future vocation.

Sincerely yours,

Donald B. Keat II, Ph.D.
Multimodal Child Psychologist

7 Training as Multimodal Treatment for Peers

The age of peer help appears to be upon us. The piecemeal way the use of peer helpers has been approached over the past 10 years may be changing. In the past, many of us, myself included, have used peer counseling on a case-by-case basis, utilizing peer helpers wherever they seemed to be needed in any particular situation. What appears to be needed is a more systematic approach to the training of peers in order to have them function more effectively in a helping role.

Over the past 10 years much of the literature has dealt with older (i.e., not elementary school) groups. Some illustrations gleaned from the college level are Brown (1965), Biehn (1972), Wrenn and Mencke (1972), and Corrigan (1974). At the high school level, peer counseling has been reported by Vriend (1969), Hamburg and Varenhorst (1972), Kramer (1974), Varenhorst (1974), Giles (1975), and Frank, Ferdinand, and Bailey (1975). Big brother or buddy programs utilizing older persons (adolescents or adults) with elementary school children have been cited by McWilliams and Finkel (1973) and Fo and O'Donnel (1974).

But these reports are not directly on the target of peer counseling with elementary school children. The dawning of this movement has only taken place in the past five years or so. There are only a few reports of work in this area: Kern and Kirby (1971), Gumaer (1973), and McCann (1975).

The purpose of this chapter is to present some gains that accrue from being a peer helper. By utilizing the multimodal treatment model, a "gains profile" will be developed to highlight many of the possible treatment gains which a person might encounter while in training to be a helper.

---

* Reprinted with changes from Elementary School Guidance and Counseling, 1976, 11, 7-13. Copyright 1976 by American Personnel and Guidance Association. Reprinted with permission.

MULTIMODAL TREATMENT

In expanding the multimodal model for work with elementary school children, I proposed enlargements for two of the modes (Keat, 1976a). The first one was the S mode to encompass School-related concerns. The second expansion was the D mode to include Diet considerations in working with children. Although the BASIC ID format is a useful one for the counselor to use in organizing cases, I found that the acronym was confusing to many of the parents to whom I was attempting to convey the multidimensional model for approaching children. Therefore, I have adapted the same modes to another acronym which is more understandable to most parents (see Chapter 8). This acronym is HELPING (Table 1-3, Chapter 1).

In organizing the benefits which accrue from peer training, this same HELPING acronym is a useful viewpiece with which to focus on the various gains the peers should experience. The following table summarizes what the various letters in the slightly revised acronym stand for as well as presents the treatment gains as a result of training.

Table 7-1
HELPING Peers

Mode	Treatment Gains
Help	Self-help Feels useful Warm fuzzies
Emotions	Feelings identified Empathy
Learn	Learning of rules, respect, rights of others
Peers, people, personal-problems	Friendship training Positive adult relationship Problem coping skills
Image (self), Interests	IALAC Interests broadened
Needs, Nourishing	Belonging to group Esteem
Guidance of acts, behaviors, consequences	Rehearse reponsible behaviors Decision-making skills Consider consequences of actions

HELPING PEERS

The summary table presented will serve as a point of departure for discussion of possible gains for a hypothetical group of peers who have undergone training. Any one individual would probably only experience some of these gains.

Help

The H in the HELPING acronym stands for Help. These are the good feelings that persons get from helping others. It is probably the core experience that underlies the "helper therapy principle" (Carkhuff, 1968, p. 123) in that "lay programs simply try to prepare people to help people." Guerney (1969, p. 247) has stated that "the helper is often himself changed for the better as a consequence of his effort."

Another benefit derived from the help one person gives to another is that the helper feels useful. The helper gets positive reinforcement from the clients (i.e., peers) with whom he/she is called upon to work. These rewards may give the peer helper something to be good at in school. For some children, this may be the only thing they're good at. Therefore, they may reap benefits in their overall attitude toward school and it may give them something positive for which to come to school. An example of this is a big child in sixth grade who was doing poorly academically and was picking on others. We used his physical prowess to help curtail the movement of a hyperactive third grader. Both children benefited; the third grader had some external control agent to help him inhibit his activities. The sixth grader used his physical skills in a constructively useful way. "Warm fuzzies" (Freed, 1973) were experienced by both of the boys.

Emotions or Empathy

The E in HELPING can stand for either Emotions or Empathy. Emotions have to do with the child's feelings. "Identifying feelings in self and others" is one of the sessions in the peer facilitator training program discussed by Gumaer (1976a). The development of a feelings vocabulary precedes the relating of these words to behaviors.

Another type of emotional gain for the helper is the energizing feeling of helping someone else. In this sense the helper gets "up" for his performance. An example of this would be the situation in which a fairly meek helper becomes more assertive when standing up for the rights of others.

Empathy has been described as walking in another's shoes. The peer has a greater probability of doing this than the adult helper who works with children, especially when skill training is used to enhance peer capability. The particular skill training used to enhance peers' capabilities should add to their potential. Some of these are based on the Carkhuff (1969a, 1969b) and Carkhuff and Bierman (1970) training model but are adopted for use with children. The basic communication skills of listening, clarifying, reflecting, and giving feedback are all parts of Gumaer's training sessions (1976). By gaining some skill in these areas, the child's ability to interact effectively with both children and adults should be enhanced.

Learn

The L in HELPING represents the Learning that takes place in schools. Specifically, learning of the three R's is relevant here. The three R's are Rules, Respect- Regard, and the Rights of others.

Learning rules for classroom discussions are an integral part of peer-facilitator programs. Gumaer delineated five basic rules for his groups. The basic rules were: "(a) one person speaks at a time; (b) raise your hand before speaking; (c) it is okay to express any thought or feeling; (d) when talking, make it brief; and (e) be a good listener" (Gumaer, 1973, p. 6). As children work with these rules, they should internalize these guidelines.

The second of the three R's stands for Respect-Regard for others. By learning to show an interest in others, a child can be perceived by his peers as exhibiting positive regard. These feelings then have a greater chance of being reciprocated.

The third R pertains to the Rights of others. If one views the group as a potential source of learning about life, then one of the gains should have to do with keeping "the faith" (Frank, Ferdinand, & Bailey, 1975) about what someone has shared with another person. Learning to keep certain information confidential can heighten others' trust in you, that is, they can talk to the trained peer without concern that their secrets will be blabbed around in a gossipy fashion.

A program which epitomizes the application of these three R's in the schools is one conceived and conducted by Mark Golanoski while he was an elementary school counseling intern in the public schools. Mark called his program a "peer umpire program." A description of this peer umpire program follows.

The peer umpire program was developed in response to a need for order and organization during the recess periods at an elementary school. Kickball was a very popular recess game. The younger children, however, demonstrated difficulty following the rules, remembering the score, and understanding when they were "safe" or "out." Due to confusion resulting in conflicts and arguments, teachers often had to pay as close attention to this recess activity as to classroom exercises.

Collaboration between the counselor and a fifth-grade teacher resulted in the names of five students being chosen as umpires. All five were enthusiastic about participating in the program. This group of fifth graders (two boys and three girls) was trained to umpire the recess kickball games of the younger children. It was felt that they could afford the time away from the classroom and would benefit a great deal from a special program in which they could develop a feeling of importance, an appropriate assertive manner, and a sense of responsibility.

Prior to initiation of the program, the umpires met for a training session in which the procedures of umpiring and the rules of the game were explained by the counselor. The umpires met as a small group each week to discuss the previous week's work and any questions or concerns they might have had. The counselor purchased several red T-shirts with the word "umpire" printed on the back. These shirts were designed to make the umpire stand out as an important figure in the game. The umpires were to wear these shirts only when they were officiating a game. Score cards were made and kept in the guidance office along with the shirts. The score cards were 4"x6" index cards marked off according to innings (as in typical baseball score cards) with a space for the final score to be tabulated and room at the bottom for the signatures of the teacher and the umpire.

A large calendar-type sign-up sheet was posted outside of the guidance office (see Table 7-2). When a teacher desired the services of an umpire, she would sign her name in the block along with the time she was taking her class outside to play the game. Teachers were asked to sign up one day before their games were going to be played so the umpires would know in the morning if they were going to work that day and could complete their school work accordingly. If an umpire could be available at the time a teacher signed for, he/she would sign his/her name underneath the teacher's and meet the class outside at the designated time. There was enough space in each block of the sign-up sheet for several teachers to sign for umpires on the same day and at the same time.

Table 7-2 - Umpire Sign Up Sheet

Monday	Tuesday	Wednesday	Thursday	Friday
Miss Hart	Mrs. Smith			Mr. Davis
1:30-2:00	2:00-2:30			12:30-1:00
Joey	Samantha			Kim
	Mrs. Jones	Mrs. Smith		
	12:15-12:45	2:00-2:30		
2	Lenny 3	Lois 4	5	6
	Mr. Davis		Miss Hart	
	12:30-1:00		1:00-1:30	
	Kim		Joey	
			Mrs. Smith	
			12:30-1:00	
9	10	11	Lenny 12	13

For this pilot program, umpires were available between 12:15 and 2:30 daily. Each umpire was permitted to work only once a day for one half-hour recess period.

An "umpire's corner" was set up in the guidance office. All equipment (shirts, score cards, pencils) was kept on a table under a collage (made by the counselor) showing pictures of umpires in action. The umpires who were working a particular day picked up the equipment first thing in the morning. The equipment was kept in the student's desk until needed and returned to the guidance office at the end of the day. This procedure eliminated the possibility of the umpires interrupting counseling sessions by going in and out of the office all day long for equipment.

From the inception of the program, the teachers received the umpires wholeheartedly. Although the teachers were still required to be outside with their class, they were free to relax somewhat and socialize with one another because the umpires were there to keep score, call the plays, and settle disputes. The umpires served as models of good sportsmanship for the younger children and brought order to their games. In addition to helping the teachers, the children involved also benefited. They got the opportunity to develop a sense of responsibility. A cake and ice cream party planned for the end of the school year served as a reward for the umpires although being a member of a "special" group with the "special" shirts and "special" responsibility appeared to be very rewarding in and of itself.

This program was piloted in one wing of a three-wing school complex. The potential for growth exists in the fact that the program's popularity spread. Teachers from other wings expressed an interest in receiving the umpire service. Other students asked the counselor for permission to become umpires. This peer umpire program could be expanded to accommodate the entire school. The further possibility existed of having the five pilot program umpires, who would be in sixth grade the following year, serve as umpire supervisors, and train a new group of fifth graders to be the umpires.

A final area of learning, but one that doesn't fit under the classic three R rubric, is that of music. Music can be used in the classroom or groups in such a way that the children learn something about life. Gumaer (1973) has used different songs to convey messages. By carefully selecting lyrics which are interesting plus have some message (e.g., "Keep a happy outlook and be good to your friends," from "Lucky Seven Sampson," Multiplication Rock, Capitol Records SJA-1174), children can have fun while incorporating worthwhile values and skills.

Peers, People, Personal-Problems

The three P's of the HELPING relationships are Peers, People (i.e., interpersonal relationships), and Personal- Problems. Gumaer (1973) starts his training sessions with get-acquainted exercises. These types of exercises form the basis for one of the three steps in "friendship training" (Keat & Guerney, 1978). The three stages in this process are meeting, greeting, and keeping friends.

1. Meeting friends.   First, children need to place themselves in situations conducive to meeting peers. This meeting scene could take place within the group, at the playground, during athletic events, or any other potential situation in which peers are drawn together.

2. Greeting children.   Once children are together, this is the stage where the "get acquainted" types of skills enter, that is, what to say in the initial encounter.

3. Keeping friends. The final stage is the crucial one of managing to keep friends once the child has them. This involves making oneself an interesting person with skills (e.g., game playing) who is fun to be with.

The interpersonal skills that children in peer training receive are helpful in getting along with others. These skills involve some of the communication activities previously discussed under Empathy. In addition, Gumaer (1973) enlarges this to include human relations with different types of persons other than those with whom a child might typically be involved. Another exposure the peer in training receives is that of supervision with an adult. In this situation, the child is working closely with an adult in a different type of relationship. Some benefits gained from his exposure are achieving a positive relationship with an adult, gaining a model with whom to identify, and receiving the support and understanding of an adult.

The final of the three P's is personal problems. At times life can be construed as a series of problems. How well we work through these various difficulties is a measure of our maturity. In this sense, how well a child can learn to cope with troubles is important. For example, I work with several families who have children who are overly concerned about going to school on the bus. A solution for one family was to have a fourth grader dropped off at the house of a sixth grader (both families are clients). The fourth grader felt more secure because of being able to go on the bus with a peer he knew. The sixth grader felt important because of his increased responsibility. Another solution to the bus problem has been to train peers (fifth and sixth graders) to monitor and help supervise the school buses. These children enjoy the power and prestige of being a helper and the children (especially the scapegoated ones) reap the benefits of a more orderly bus ride (not to mention the improved emotional status of many of the bus drivers).

Image - Interests

The I in HELPING represents two dimensions, self- Image and the children's Interests. A positive self-image is probably the one most important thing for a child to possess. It is good to feel that I am Loveable and Capable" (IALAC) (Simon, 1973). As a child helps others, he/she should feel more worthwhile. Self-disclosure is a procedure typically utilized in peer training groups (Gumaer, 1973). As a child learns to share "secrets" (Gumaer,

1976a), he/she can learn to feel more comfortable with others. With increasing openness, a child becomes less self-centered and increases his/her concern for others (Goodman, 1972). For some children, a useful way of introducing this concept is through the use of the "inner circle strategy" (Lazarus, 1971). By combining this procedure with "secret pooling," the therapist can get the group members to share their secrets more readily (Keat, 1974a).

The area of interests has to do with the child acquiring a variety of interests so that he/she can talk more readily about such things as books or movies. In addition, a child who has a broad range of skills in peer games (e.g., cards) is usually more welcome as a group member.

Needs

The N in HELPING represents the Nourishing and Nurturant Needs that are met for the peer helper. At a basic level, a person, when needed, feels pleasure in task involvement. To be nurturant means "to reach out in a responsible and sometimes fatherly (or motherly) manner" (Goodman, 1972, p. 48). There are at least two possible ways of considering the aspects of needs. One is to use Maslow's (1970) need hierarchy as a way of considering some needs. The first two types of needs (i.e., physiological and safety) are probably not relevant here. But the other three are. For example, the child's love needs can be partially met by belonging to a group in which positive feelings are given and received. Esteem needs were discussed under the last mode (image-self). These can be enhanced from experiencing the acceptance and respect of others. In this manner, some children may attain a higher level of self-actualization or self-fulfillment. I've had children tell me that they want to do something like what I do when they grow up because they feel they can help others. By trying this type of behavior out in a group of peers, they can field test their hopes and dreams.

A second way of perceiving the possible gains from experiencing group training is to consider some of the developmental tasks for "middle childhood" (Havighurst, 1953). Some of the relevant gains here could be learning the necessary physical skills for ordinary games (number 1), building a positive self-concept (number 2), learning to get along with age mates (number 3), developing concepts necessary for everyday living (number 6), achieving personal independence (number 8) or group training as a step toward maturity, and developing appropriate attitudes toward social groups and institutions (number 9).

Guidance of Acts, Behaviors, and Consequences

The final letter of HELPING represents the G in Guidance of acts, behaviors, and consequences. Acting appropriately can be one of the benefits derived from the training. As peers prepare, conduct, and are accountable for their group meetings, they also develop a sense of responsibility (Frank et al., 1975).

There are a variety of behaviors which can be affected. As a result of some of the basic peer group training in counseling skills, such things as attending and eye contact should be improved. The importance of modeling should also be stressed. When a child sees and hears his peers do or say something, it is often somewhat more believable because they're in the same boat. In such procedures as role playing as discussed by Gumaer (1973), the children behaviorally rehearse acts which should generalize to other life situations. In their training of fifth and sixth graders, Kern and Kirby (1971) cite that they actually consider techniques of changing behavior (à la Dreikurs). Gumaer (1973) mentions the development of decision-making skills as a topic in one of the peer training sessions. These types of abilities should have generalization outside the group.

Finally, there are outcomes or consequences of the preceding acts and behaviors. As a result of these activities, the peer helper should learn to act more responsibly, to develop good attending behaviors, to practice appropriate behaviors for a variety of situations, to learn some techniques for influencing the behavior of others, and to internalize some decision-making procedures.

SUMMARY

This chapter presented the multimodal model for viewing the gains which accrue from being trained as a peer helper. By utilizing the HELPING acronym, the leader was led through a multimodal treatment profile which outlined the possible gains to persons trained in the helping skills. If the peer helper can attain some of these skills or reap some of the benefits discussed throughout this chapter, then he/she will have a basis for feeling better about helping himself/herself, others, and life in general. To be a helper in a HELPING relationship can be one of the greatest rewards in life.

8 Multimodal Therapy With Parents: Helping Your Child

As I am confronted each day with the task of HELPING children and their parents, the crucial question always in the foreground of my mind is how can I HELP these parents, this family, and this child? The more basic question, of course, is how can I train these parents in HELPING their child(ren)?

MULTIMODAL THERAPY

The purpose of this chapter is to share with you my eyeglasses with which to look at the parents and children with whom you are called upon to work. Although I have been using the multimodal lens for several years in working with children and families (Keat, 1976a), in working with parents who have never heard of Freud's Id (ego, superego), it seemed that another acronym from their background might be more understandable and more effective. Therefore, I have adapted the same seven areas of the BASIC ID to the previously discussed acronym, i.e., HELPING. My instructions to parents initially go something like the following:

HELPING YOUR CHILD
(INSTRUCTIONS FOR PARENTS)

The important question to always keep in mind is "How can I help my child?" HELPING persons is the key. Keeping this word HELPING in mind, take each letter and use it to look at your child, that is, H stands for the Health of your child. If you have any concerns about this area or any of the others we will discuss, then we will figure out some activity or procedure to help in the particular area. The E represents the first letter of the word Emotions or feelings of your child. The L is the first letter in the word

Learning. Do you have any worries about how your child is Learning in school? P represents the first letter in People or Personal relationships. I stands for your child's Imagination or his/her land of make believe. The N represents the Need to know. This is the child's process of thinking about himself and others. The final letter, G, represents the Guidance of your child's actions, behaviors, and consequences (Guidance of A, B, Cs).

By asking yourself, "How can I HELP my child?" and by keeping what area each of the first letters of the word HELPING stands for, you will be able to more effectively focus your efforts on the particular area(s) with which he/she needs the most help.

Table 8-1 summarizes the HELPING areas and the related procedures which can be used under each of them. After spending a session or two with the parents, I usually give them a copy of Table 8-1. From this table, we select the procedures (underline them in red) which we feel will be useful for them in HELPING their child. Then we rank order the modes and start with their zone of greatest concern.

Table 8-1
HELPING Your Child
Procedures for Effective Parenting

Health

Diet therapy
Panic Book

Emotions-Feelings

Relaxation exercises
Assertive training
Directed muscular activity
Games and play activities
Emotional education

Learning-School

Restructuring environment
Timeout
Perceptual-motor training programs
Gross motor coordination activities
Speech therapy
Tutoring

People-Personal Relationships

Communication training
Family meetings
Sibling interactions ("Instant Replay")
Friendship training
Big brother (sister) or buddy programs

Imagination

Self-esteem enhancement
Emotive (hero) imagery
Thought stopping
Time projection

Need to Know - Think

Irrational self-talk (mistaken ideas)
Decision making, problem solving
Bibliotherapy
Values clarification
Sex education

Guidance of Actions, Behaviors, and Consequences

Behavior rehearsal (modeling)
Behavioral contracting
Job jar
Self-control (inhibition training)
Natural or logical consequences
Bathroom technique
Saturday box

In order to work with the selected procedures, you have several avenues of approach. One is that you discuss and directly instruct parents in the procedures which can be helpful with their concerns. For example, if they want to know what the "Saturday box" is, you would explain that there is a specified day (e.g., Saturday) at which time the box can be opened. The box contains such things as toys or clothes which have not been put away by a predetermined time (e.g., bedtime). If these things are not picked up by bedtime, then the parent picks them up and puts them in the Saturday box. They are then unavailable to the child until the box is opened. Once children have lost some valued toys or a particular pair of shoes they wanted to wear, they generally learn to pick up their things. In this fashion, you are a teacher-clinician who is instructing the parent in new procedures for handling their child.

Or you can use the homework reading process. I typically give the parents a copy of the chapter from a book (Keat & Guerney, 1978) which addresses the particular mode about which they are concerned. They take this home, read it, apply some of the ideas, come to the next session and discuss how it worked. We usually focus on one selected mode for several weeks before going on to the second zone in their rank order of concerns. You can also select a book which you feel fits into the parent's value framework (see Appendix B). For example, if the problem is primarily one in which the child exhibits irresponsible behaviors and the family is democratic philosophically, then you could recommend that they buy or borrow Dinkmeyer and McKay (1973) or Dreikurs and Soltz (1964). If you think they could benefit from direct technique ideas, then I would recommend Patterson (1971). With regard to the buying or borrowing issue, if your clients can afford to buy their own books, this is a good procedure. If they can't, then my practice is to let them borrow my books. I have an active lending library for parents in which I keep multiple copies of the cited books available (or your clinic or school should have a lending library). You can note that most of these books are about parenting although some of them are for the parents' self-help (e.g., Lazarus & Fay, 1975). There is some risk involved in this because often parents do not return books. At one stage last year I had over 100 books which had not been returned. I sent a letter to the effect that "I enjoy sharing my books as I do my friends, asking only that you treat them well and see them safely home. If you happen to have borrowed one or some of my books and are now done with the books, please return them to me at your earliest convenience. You can do this by bringing them to your appointment, dropping them off with my receptionist, or mailing them. Thank you."

For those parents who are not readers, the auditory mode may be utilizable. For this, I have a lending library of cassette tapes available. Some examples are: for adult relaxation (Lazarus, 1970, 1975); for child relaxation (Keat, 1977, tape 2); for divorced parents (Gardner, 1975); for procedures about enhancing self-esteem (Keat, 1977, tape 1); or for discipline techniques (Keat, 1977, tape 3). Many people now have cassette machines in their homes. If they do not, I keep some ready to lend.

The word HELPING is a useful way of looking at and attempting to understand where parents can most effectively work with and help their child. It should be remembered, nevertheless, that with some cases an intervention in only one or two zones may be needed. For example, what a child may need could be a big brother or sister and therefore the only mode dealt with would be the People- Personal relationships zone.

Two additional points should be made: (1) in order to have lasting therapeutic effects, the more modes you work in the greater positive impact you will have, and (2) almost every parent and child can benefit from doing at least one thing in each mode.

A CASE ILLUSTRATION: THE HURTING FAMILY

The following represents an illustration of work with a family which I am currently seeing (The Hurting Family). In this situation there is an intervention being made in every zone.

Table 8-2
HELPING Program for the Hurting Family

Area	Problem	Procedure
Health	Poor diet	Diet therapy
Emotions	Too tense	Relaxation training
Learning	Reading below grade level	Reading tutor
People	Household chores	Family meeting (Job jar)

Area	Problem	Procedure
Imagination	Fears traveling in family car	Emotive (hero) imagery
Need to Know	Sibling rivalry	Bibliotherapy
Guidance of A, B, Cs	Chores, personal responsibility	Behavioral contracting

Health

Health is the state of children's physical well being. Both physical exercise and diet are relevant here. In this case the emphasis is on: (1) making parent and child aware of dietary considerations, (2) monitoring food intake for a while, (3) changing the child's diet. Regarding number 1, a useful little brochure is published by the Department of Agriculture. It is available (free) from Consumer Information (Pueblo, Colorado 81009) and is entitled, The Thing the Professor Forgot. Children enjoy reviewing food groups (i.e., meat, vegetables and fruits, cereals and breads, and milk) with Oonoose Q. Eckwoose who is a professor of "foodology." The second step (i.e., monitoring) can take place by having the parent and/or child keep track of what they eat for breakfast, lunch, dinner, and snacks. Once this is done, they can note particular lacks (for example, no vegetables) or excesses (for example, too many sweets) in the child's diet. The final goal, changing the child's diet, is crucial in reducing the amount of "junk" foods taken in or in increasing the number of wholesome foods in their diet. For guidelines about diet, I often refer them to Feingold (1975), Reuben (1975), or Stevens, Stevens, and Stoner (1977).

Emotions

Relaxation training is one of the best antidotes for anxiety. In this mode I train the child in appropriate breathing, tension-relaxation of various muscles in the body, combining breathing and tension-relaxation exercises, and the use of various pleasant pictures to flash on their mind (Keat, 1974a). There are detailed relaxation directions available (e.g., Keat, 1974b) as well as tapes. For children I now use the Self-relaxation Program for Children (Keat, 1977, tape 2). See Appendix A for the instructions. For the parents, who may well need relaxation training themselves (if only to enhance their modeling impact), I lend them a copy of the Lazarus (1970 or 1975) relaxation directions.

Learning (School)

Almost everyone can benefit from receiving some specialized help. A tutor can help a child to remediate a specific deficit. In addition, it should be kept in mind that the person should also be capable of forming a positive relationship with the child in order to enhance motivation (which is sometimes more problematic than the specific skill itself). As a therapist, you should be able to provide referral to such a tutor for the parent. In this particular case, reading tutoring was used in order to bring the child up to appropriate grade-level functioning.

People-Personal Relationships

The use of "family council meetings" can be an effective procedure with most families once the children are at least four years of age. Family meeting procedures are thoroughly described for parents in Dinkmeyer and McKay (1973), Dreikurs, Gould, and Corsini (1974), Corsini and Painter (1975).

The three basic steps are (from Keat & Guerney, 1978):

1. Setting a time and place. For example this family chose Sunday evening, 6-7 p.m., after the meal and before the favorite T.V. programs started. The place was around the dinner table.

2. Rules. Keep simple rules and limits, i.e. only allowing one person to speak at a time and listening to each other.

3. Order of balance. To review old business and introduce new business. An example of one procedure used in this family was the "job jar" (listed under Guidance of A, B, Cs). This procedure is described by Dinkmeyer and McKay (1973). Briefly, it is a jar which contains slips of paper with jobs (household chores) written on them. Once these chores (jobs) are decided upon at a family meeting, then they are written down and placed in the jar. Each person then draws from the jar, taking turns, until all the jobs are taken. In this way, the jobs are distributed around the family by chance. Most children enjoy a lottery and when handled in this fashion the children cannot blame their parents for being assigned a particular job. It was just (bad) luck or fate.

Imagination

Emotive or hero imagery can be useful when the parents want their child to become engaged in something of which they are afraid. In this case, a 10-year-old child feared traveling in the family car. The child imagined a series of scenes in which the boy and his father proudly showed the automobile to the boy's favorite T.V. character (Steve Austin, The Six Million Dollar Man). Then the child imagined that Steve was excited and asked to go for a ride in the car. The group then went through a series of scenes building up to a chase in which the boy and his father were riding in the car in pursuit of international spies. After several scenes like this, the child's tension was lessened and he was able (with more ease) to go on family outings in the car (as Steve or himself).

Need to Know - Think

Bibliotherapy is the procedure in which the parents read books to their child (or the child reads them) and the stories have emotional messages, learnings, or moral lessons. The procedure is to read the story in the regular fashion, stop and discuss things as they arise, and then carry on a discussion after the story is completed. The key is to choose the book that has a meaningful message for the child (see Baruth & Phillips, 1976). In this situation one of the topics of concern was sibling rivalry. Therefore, the book entitled Instant Replay (Bedford, 1974) was used (see under People mode) because it depicts a five-step sequence to help parents deal with sibling conflicts. Appendix C lists additional useful books for children. For adolescents, see Appendix D.

Guidance of Actions, Behaviors, Consequences

Behavioral contracts are useful procedures. The contract usually entails the delineation of what a child is going to do and what he/she will get if the behaviors are carried out. The following example is drawn from the case illustration. This contract represents an agreement between the parents and Peter. The program included the behaviors listed on the left of Table 8-3. In addition, it should be noted that different activities are weighted (valued) with various numbers. These values can be arrived at by discussing them with the child. Some things (e.g., getting along with brothers/sisters) are obviously more difficult than others (e.g., drying the pots).

Parents differ on their views about having an allowance being based on what the child does around the house. Some parents think that an allowance should be given to a child because he/she exists. Others feel that it should be based upon some responsible performance in the home. I am in agreement with the second stance and feel that "purse power" should be started as soon as possible - that is, about age five (Robertiello, 1975). It also seems that most children feel that they should do something to get a reward. On a recent "Wonderama" T.V. show, about 97% of the children polled said that they should do jobs in order to get an allowance.

In addition to basic household chores and personal responsibilities, children can have special extra jobs which are paid activities. Such chores as cutting the grass, cleaning the car, shoveling the snow, babysitting for younger brothers and sisters can be rewarded with money. A benefit of children having their own money is that they can learn its value and they learn savings habits. Then when parents and children go to a store, they know that they can buy whatever they have enough for. If they want something that costs $3.50 and they only have $1.75, they learn that it is their responsibility to have enough money and they cannot ask their parents for it. This practice significantly cuts down on public hassles between parent and child.

In rewarding children with allowances and using a cost system, it is important that the child get something for his/her efforts and that he/she doesn't lose all of his/her money. It is usually more helpful to be encouraging in some way, even if the reward is small.

The contract between Peter and his parents represents a combination of all these elements, that is, household chores, personal responsibilities, a weighting system based upon the difficulty of the chore or duty, a daily checklist, and a response-cost reward system which pays off according to the number of points which he earns. For the week cited, he earned 39 points and therefore got $.75.

Table 8-3
Peter's Program of Chores and Responsibilities

	Weighting	M	T	W	T	F	S	SUN
Clears table	(1)	✓	✓	✓		✓	✓	
Practices piano	(2)	✓		✓	✓	✓		✓
Dries pots	(1)	✓	✓		✓	✓		
Gets along well with brothers/sisters in evening	(3)	✓			✓			✓
Brushes teeth	(1)	✓	✓	✓	✓	✓		
Is in bed by 9 p.m.	(1)	✓	✓	✓	✓	✓		
Day's total		9	4	5	8	6	2	5
Week's total =		39	(Gets $.75)					

Rewards:

1. If Peter (10 years old) gets 57-63 points, he gets full allowance (i.e., $1.50 per week).
2. If he gets 50-57 points, he gets $.25 off ($1.25).
3. If he gets 43-49 points, he gets $.50 off ($1.00).
4. If he gets 36-42 points, he gets $.75 off ($.75).
5. If he gets 29-35 points, he gets $.50.

SUMMARY

This chapter has presented the multimodal approach for therapists to use in their work with parents who want to be involved in HELPING their children. After the more general HELPING summary table of 34 procedures was presented, the therapist was taken through an actual case with illustrations of techniques from each of the modes. By utilizing this practical eclectic approach (i.e., whatever procedures are useful), therapists should be able to effect more lasting changes in HELPING their clients.

9 Multimodal Assessment: The Classroom Ecology Schedule

The school is now being recognized as a broad environment which influences a child's behavioral, emotional, sensory, self-concept, social, and physical as well as the traditionally emphasized area of cognitive development. Such awareness of the school's wide range of influence was identified by the American Association of School Administrators (1966) when they delineated the following imperatives:

1. To make urban life rewarding and satisfying

2. To prepare people for the world of work

3. To discover and nurture creative talent

4. To strengthen the moral fabric of society

5. To deal constructively with psychological tensions

6. To keep democracy working

7. To make intelligent use of natural resources

8. To make the best use of leisure time

9. To work with other people of the world for human betterment

Such a list makes it clear that our contemporary educational institutions must go beyond the traditional three R's and provide features which have a positive influence on the pupil's whole self. That is, to educate the "whole child."

Attending to the educational needs of children, as implied by the goals

---

* This chapter, which was co-authored by Richard D. Judah, is a complete version of an abridged article, from Elementary School Guidance and Counseling, 1977, 12, 97-106. Reprinted by permission.

outlined above, requires that those involved in the educational process provide conditions which facilitate the kinds of learning that increase the pupil's repertoire of skills in enhancing his/her life and the lives of fellow human beings. Such a task requires careful consideration of the educaional institution as not just a place, but as an environment which, like most other kinds of environments, has many features and characteristics upon which the child's successful functioning and development are contingent. The enormity and complexity of this task also requires a systematic, nonrandom kind of attention to the ecological conditions of the pupil's institutional environment, which in turn necessitates the utilization of sound conceptual guidelines and observational skills. In short, what is really required to implement and insure educational climates conducive to total pupil growth are mechanisms for systematically observing and evaluating the characteristics of the institutional world in which the person (child) goes about his/her process of learning.

MULTIMODAL CLASSROOM ASSESSMENT

The multimodal approach holds much promise as a vehicle for filling the void in the availability of means for meeting the concerns described above. Such a categorial model extends far beyond the sphere of psychotherapy and has relevance for a wide range of disciplines relative to the assessment and enhancement of human functioning. Indeed, it may very well be that the modalities identified by Lazarus (1976) cut across nearly the whole gamut of human functioning, creating a scheme which is limited only by the imagination of the person applying it. For example, one of the authors (Keat, 1976a) has adapted the model for providing therapeutic assistance to children and adolescents (Chapters 5 and 6). In addition, he has utilized the approach for identifying gains accruing from peer treatment (see Chapter 7); Keat and Guerney (1978) have applied it to parent education (see also Chapter 8); Gerler and Keat (1977) have employed the model for multimodal education (see Chapter 10). Additional applications for the model have been developed and include such considerations as helping learning-disabled children (Keat & Hatch, in press) and personal growth from a multimodal standpoint (Chapter 2). The method to be described next extends its use to perhaps the most important environment for the educational process - the classroom.

The multimodal model in the context of this chapter is seen as a promising conceptual device for assessing classroom ecology, that is, systematically examining or observing the impact or influence of the relationship between pupils and classroom environment on the kind of developmental imperatives outlined earlier. The creation of such a device has been accomplished by organizing observations of classrooms across seven categories nearly identical to those identified by Lazarus (1976) and adapted for application to child psychology by Keat (1976a). These categories, identified here as environmental modes, comprise an assessment device known as the Classroom Ecology Schedule designed primarily to assist elementary school classroom observers (e.g., psychologists, counselors, social workers, and administrators) in organizing their perceptions of a given classroom into some meaningful

Gestalt, whereby they might develop some relevant conclusions regarding the impact of the classroom, its activities, people, and conditons, on the overall purposes it serves. It is clear that such a device has potential value as a method for evaluating classroom climate as a prelude to initiating sound classroom practices (see Chapter 10).

The dimensions or modes of the Classroom Ecology Schedule (CES) are globally defined in the following manner:

Behavioral environment - The behavioral mode refers to the kinds of overt, ongoing activities in the classroom, the behavioral activity and demeanor of the children as well as the teacher's mechanisms or methods for enhancing positive behavior and alleviating negative kinds of behavior. Also included are items which are designed to help the observer focus in on any particular children who may stand out in terms of special characteristics. Items 1 through 5 and 40 through 45 address this modal configuration.

Affective environment - This mode refers to the psychological tone or emotional mood of the classroom. Items are designed to assist the observer in targeting in on such features as the general mood of the children, the kind of feelings exhibited by the teacher, and the opportunity or availability of activities for emotional growth. The items which reflect upon this zone are 6 through 9 and 46 through 48.

Sensory environment - Herein items are designed to stimulate observation and yield information on the perceptual and other sensory (e.g., visual, tactile, auditory) elements of the classroom environment that influence pupil growth in both cognitive and emotional spheres. Such factors as noise level, lighting, and ventilation are seen as falling under this rubric, which includes items 10 through 18 and 49 and 50.

Imagery environment - Items falling under this modal category relate primarily to the opportunity for children to utilize their imaginations and creative capacities to enhance cognitive and expressive development. Such items are considered as crucial to the developmental process, yet often seem to be overlooked as an educational vehicle for growth. The items related to this zone are 19 through 22.

Cognitive environment - This category very generally relates to the identification of elements of the classroom that revolve around the learning process. This zone might also be referred to as the instructional climate and includes items that cover instructional methods, pupil response, and identification of pupils with learning problems. Items 23 through 28, 51 and 52 deal with this mode.

Interpersonal environment - Dealing primarily with the "social climate," items here cover global observations of peer interactions, teacher-pupil relationships, and the identification of pupils who might act as a classroom "catalysts" for positive or negative classroom activity. The relevant items herein are 29 through 35 and 53 through 55.

Dietary, Physical, Recreational environment - This mode refers primarily to the attention given to the physical needs and development of the students. Items relate to availability of activities that contribute to sound physical development and personal care. Importance is also attached to education for nutritional wisdom and identification of pupils who are in need for special attention because of physical or medical reasons. Items covering this zone are 36 through 39 and 56 through 59.

Table 9-1 provides an overview of the CES. By looking at this table, you can quickly determine the BASIC ID environmental modes, the items that cover these particular zones, and see an illustrative item drawn from the scale.

Table 9-1
Classroom Ecology Schedule

Rating Scale: Strongly Agree (4); Agree (3); Disagree (2);
                 Strongly Disagree (1); Non-Response (0)

Environment	Items	Sample Items
Behavioral	1-5, 40-45	2. The children's activity and behavior seem productive.
Affective	6-9, 46-48	7. Children are encouraged to express their positive feelings.
Sensory	10-18, 49-50	12. Seating arrangement is such that children and teachers have positive contact and communication.
Imagery	19-22	19. Children seem to be encouraged to engage in imaginative/creative activities (art, music, plays, etc.).
Cognitive	23-28, 51-52	27. Materials and instruction are presented as having generalization outside the classroom.
Interpersonal	29-35, 53-55	35. Teacher makes use of the classroom meeting approach.

| Dietary, Physical, Recreational | 36-39, 56-59 | 39. Recreational activities are systematically designed to contribute to children's physical well-being. |

The CES is a 39 item, five-point rating scale with item responses ranging from Strongly Agree (a rating of 4) to Strongly Disagree (a rating of 1) with a rating of 0 being given for an item about which the observer cannot respond or is unsure. A total is obtained by adding the ratings of 39 items; a higher score reflects a more favorable classroom climate. An additional 20 items are included to provide for further comment and qualitative data. Items 40 through 59 allow the observer to incorporate more individualistic data into the classroom picture, that is, data can be gathered on children who are typically referred and thus require specific observations (e.g., disruptive, hyperactive, etc.). The completion of all items on the scale may, however, require more time than the observer has or may entail repeated observations over a period of time. If such is the case, many of the items can be completed through interview or inquiry via the teacher. Being unable to complete all items, however, does not detract from the usefulness of the schedule. Even partially completed, the CES provides an adequate means of gaining data and recording impressions of classroom environments as well as individuals who comprise the particular group.

Table 9-2 presents the entire CES, that is, items 1 through 39 (rated) and 40 through 59 (non-rated).

Table 9-2
Classroom Ecology Schedule

Date _____   Teacher _____

School _____   Number of Pupils _____

Developmental level (age or grade) _____

Period of Observation (Date and times) _____

Please respond as accurately and completely as possible to the items below by circling the most appropriate responses. Circle 4 if you Strongly Agree; 3 if you Agree; 2 if you Disagree, and 1 if you Strongly Disagree. If you are unsure about the statement or cannot respond, circle 0.

	Strongly Agree	Agree	Disagree	Strongly Disagree	No Response
1. The children's activity level is generally appropriate for this age level.	4	3	2	1	0

	Strongly Agree	Agree	Dis-agree	Strongly Dis-agree	No Re-sponse
2. Generally, the children's activity and behavior seem productive.	4	3	2	1	0
3. The children in class respond positively to the teacher's instructions and requests.	4	3	2	1	0
4. The pupils seem to enjoy participation in classroom activities.	4	3	2	1	0
5. Most of the students seem able to cope with classroom demands.	4	3	2	1	0
6. The teacher's manner appears to be generally warm and positive.	4	3	2	1	0
7. Children are encouraged to express their positive feelings.	4	3	2	1	0
8. Children are encouraged to express their negative feelings.	4	3	2	1	0
9. The mood of the classroom seems comfortable and conducive to learning and growth.	4	3	2	1	0
10. Lighting is appropriate and good for learning.	4	3	2	1	0
11. The colors of the room are pleasant, not too dreary or too overstimulating.	4	3	2	1	0
12. Seating arrangement is such that children and teacher have positive contact and communication.	4	3	2	1	0
13. Classroom displays and decorations are appealing/interesting.	4	3	2	1	0
14. There does not seem to be any seriously distracting source of noise.	4	3	2	1	0
15. Educational/instructional materials are well-organized and properly stored.	4	3	2	1	0

	Strongly Agree	Agree	Dis-agree	Strongly Dis-agree	No Re-sponse
16. Materials are stored so as not to distract when not in use.	4	3	2	1	0
17. Spaces for "time-out" or pupil privacy are provided.	4	3	2	1	0
18. The general appearance of the classroom is inviting.	4	3	2	1	0
19. Children seem to be encouraged to engage in imaginative/creative activities (art, music, plays, etc.).	4	3	2	1	0
20. Teacher seems to offer encourage-ment and praise to children frequently.	4	3	2	1	0
21. Creative/imaginative activities are reality oriented.	4	3	2	1	0
22. Children are encouraged to use their unique assets and abilities.	4	3	2	1	0
23. Teacher expresses self in an understable manner.	4	3	2	1	0
24. The teacher presents him/herself in a manner that promotes learning.	4	3	2	1	0
25. Pupils seem to respond favorably to instruction and related materials.	4	3	2	1	0
26. The teacher seems to approach instruction with interest and enthusiasm.	4	3	2	1	0
27. Materials and instruction are presented as having generali-zation outside the classroom.	4	3	2	1	0
28. Instruction and related activities are goal-oriented.	4	3	2	1	0
29. Children seem to get along well in the classroom.	4	3	2	1	0
30. Children seem to get along well during recess, lunch and other times when away from class-room.	4	3	2	1	0

	Strongly Agree	Agree	Dis-agree	Strongly Dis-agree	No Re-sponse
31. Children seem to be offered the opportunity and encouraged to share thoughts and feelings as a group.	4	3	2	1	0
32. Practice in group problem-solving is provided.	4	3	2	1	0
33. There is frequent opportunity for children to positively interact with each other and enhance their interpersonal skills.	4	3	2	1	0
34. Supervision of small-group activity is appropriate for children of this age level.	4	3	2	1	0
35. Teacher makes use of the class-room meeting approach.	4	3	2	1	0
36. Opportunity is regularly provided for exercise.	4	3	2	1	0
37. Curriculum in the classroom in-cludes topics related to self-care (e.g., grooming-health) and nutrition.	4	3	2	1	0
38. The curriculum includes education regarding alcohol/drug abuse.	4	3	2	1	0
39. Recreational activities are system-matically designed to contribute to children's physical well-being.	4	3	2	1	0

(Optional) Please respond to the following items by checking or circling the most appropriate response and/or providing comment where requested.

40.   Identify primary mechanism teacher utilizes to maintain classroom discipline (more than one may be checked):

Positive reinforcement   Negative reinforcement   Punishment

Logical consequences   Unable to identify   Other (describe)

_____

_____

41. Who initiates classroom activities?

Teacher   Pupils   Both teacher and pupils

42. Check any of the following in which you notice pupils <u>consistently</u> engaged:

Children out of seats   Disruptive talking   Arguing   Fighting

Disruptive habits (rocking, head banging)   Crying or whining

Teasing   Throwing objects   Bothering others

Other (describe) _____

_____

43. Do you notice any children who seem more active or aggressive in comparison to the other children in the classroom? If so, describe the child and in what way his/her behavior deviates from the other pupils.

_____

_____

44. Do you notice any children who might have behavioral characteristics which are outstanding in either a positive or negative sense? (e.g., hyperactive. Please describe.

_____

_____

45. Describe any child (or children) who seems to be having difficulty in handling classroom activities.

_____

_____

46. Do any of the children in the class exhibit any of the following characteristics? If so, check and describe child in space provided.

Fearful   Tense   Withdrawn   Hostile

_____

_____

47. Check or circle any of the following which, according to your frame of reference, describes the manner in which the teacher presents him/herself.

Friendly	Angry	Relaxed	Rigid	Caring
Punitive	Indifferent	Unfriendly	Cold	
Authoritarian	Abrasive	Humorous	Warm	
Rewarding	Fair	Democratic	Pleasant	Deadpan

48. Are there any children who strike you as outstanding in terms of the affect (or lack of) that they exhibit? If so, describe.

_____

_____

49. Identify particular kind of class grouping(s):

Self-contained   Open   Team teaching   Ungraded

Homogeneous (if checked, in what respect?) _____

_____

_____

50. Identify any physical classroom characteristics that might inhibit academic or emotional growth.

_____

_____

51. Are there any particular pupils who seem to have special creative abilities? If so, describe.

_____

_____

52. Are there any children who are identified as having any kind of learning problems? If so, are they provided with appropriate kinds of support and academic attention?

_____

_____

53. Are there any pupils who seem to have characteristics which make them a focal point of attention in the group in either a positive or negative sense? Describe any leaders, scapegoats, etc.

_____

_____

54.   Are there any children who seem to be "natural helpers"? If so,
       describe.

       _____

       _____

55.   Are pupils heterogeneous or homogeneous in terms of cultural, social,
       or racial background? If homogeneous, describe how they are so on
       back of page.

               Yes   No   Can't tell

56.   Are there any children in the class who appear either grossly
       overweight or undernourished? If so, identify.

       _____

       _____

57.   Are there any children who have physical handicaps?   Yes   No

       If yes, identify.   _____

       _____

58.   How are the children with physical disabilities provided for in terms of
       special assistance (i.e., prosthetics, special privileges, teacher-aides,
       etc.)? Please identify.

       _____

59.   Are any pupils assigned special seats on the basis of behavioral or
       physical difficulties? If so, describe.

       _____

60.   Additional comments. _____

       _____

       _____

       _____

SUMMARY

Multimodal assessment of a child's classroom environment is a vital step
before making meaningful interventions with individuals or groups. By
investigating the Behavioral, Affective, Sensory, Imagery, Cognitive,
Interpersonal and Dietary components of the classroom, one can obtain a
more complete picture of the school environment. The Classroom Ecology

Schedule is presented as a means for making such a comprehensive evaluation
of the school situation.   It provides a systematic way to organize the
multimodal elements observed in the classroom.   Based upon this evaluation,
the observer can then make more valid recommendations for particular
classroom interventions in specific modes.   Just what one can do in the zone
of need is the topic of the next chapter.

10 Multimodal Education: The Basic Id in the Elementary Classroom

In recent years terms such as "psychological education" (Ivey & Alschuler, 1973) and "confluent education" (Brown, 1971) have been added to the vocabularies of professionals working in elementary schools. The use of these terms has signaled a new or renewed attempt by educators to affect more than the cognitive aspects of children's functioning.

The BASIC ID model developed by Lazarus (1973) and written about in this book may help to guide educators in their continuing efforts to increase the scope and impact of elementary school instruction. Each of these aspects of human functioning should be part of a comprehensive instructional program at the elementary school level. The elementary school should help children develop and practice new behaviors, experience the joy of expressing feelings in a nonjudgmental environment, become more aware of bodily sensations, cultivate mental images helpful in reducing anxiety and fear, examine fundamental values, attitudes and beliefs, understand the process of establishing and maintaining positive interpersonal relationships, and know how drugs and diet may affect an individual's emotional and perceptual experiences.

The intent of this chapter is to identify strategies and processes that teachers may employ to touch those areas of children's functioning enumerated in the BASIC ID framework. Accordingly, this chapter borrows further from Lazarus and uses the term "multimodal" to identify a collection of educational strategies teachers can use to effect the BASIC ID of the elementary school classroom. In addition, Appendix E will provide additional useful information about particular materials for and approaches to multimodal education.

---

*This article was co-authored by Edwin R. Gerler, Jr. It is adapted from Multimodal education: Treating the "BASIC ID" of the elementary classroom. The Humanist Educator, 1977, 15, 148-154. Copyright (1977) American Personnel & Guidance Association. Reprinted by permission.

MULTIMODAL EDUCATION

The following table presents an overview of what is to follow. For each of the BASIC ID modes on the left, an illustrative program (e.g., <u>DUSO</u>, Dinkmeyer, 1970, 1973) and/or an approach (e.g., Relaxation training, <u>Keat</u>, 1977) is presented. This summary table does not present all of the procedures discussed, but gives you a visual account of several of the major ones for each mode.

Table 10-1
Multimodal Education

<u>Mode</u>	<u>Illustrative</u> <u>Program</u> <u>or</u> <u>Approach</u>
Behavior	DUSO Assertiveness Training (AT)
Affect	Human Development Program Relaxation Training
Sensation	Music Art Biofeedback
Imagery	Imagery Training IALAC
Cognition	Values Clarification Bibliotherapy (e.g., death, divorce)
Interpersonal relations	Transactional Analysis (TA) Friendship Training
Drugs-Diet	Drug Education Diet Information

Behavior

Multimodal education can help children to explore their current behaviors and to develop new behavioral repertoires to replace less effective patterns of behavior. Educators who accept Havighurst's developmental task concept (1953) see the importance of giving children opportunities to experiment with behaviors needed for new developmental stages.

Modeling and role playing are examples of strategies that allow children to explore and learn new behaviors. Although many commercial and noncommercial educational programs suggest and encourage these activities,

Dinkmeyer's (1970), 1973) program entitled Developing Understanding of Self and Others (DUSO) provides excellent modeling and role playing opportunities for elementary schoolchildren.   DUSO consists of two kits: the first is designed for children in kindergarten through second grade; the second is used with children in grades three and four (see Appendix E).

At the program's center is the puppet, "DUSO the Dolphin," who narrates most of the recorded stories incorporated into the program and who is a model of self-confidence for children.   Generally, children become strongly attached to this puppet and may ask as to its whereabouts on days when the puppet is absent from an activity.   Another puppet, "Flopsie the Flounder," is an indecisive, unsure character who provides an identification model for shy, withdrawn children.   "Coho" is a puppet who at first appears rather insensitive but later models a more accepting and understanding role.   In addition to providing children with the opportunity to observe models, the DUSO program also provides them with occasions to practice many behaviors through role-playing activities involving hand puppets.

DUSO activities exemplify the kinds of modeling and role-playing strategies that elementary school teachers might use to help children practice and learn a variety of behaviors.   Other programs with narrower objectives than DUSO have been created to help children practice and learn specific repertoires of behaviors.   Bower, Amatea, and Anderson (1976), for example, have developed a program aimed at helping shy children acquire assertive behaviors.   This training program involves children in such activities as discussion, behavioral rehearsals, videotaped reinforcement procedures, and real-life tryouts of assertive behaviors.

Rashbaum-Selig (1976) has also developed an assertion training program that can be used with children.   This program consists of about 10 sessions and involves children in a variety of activities.   Early in the program children are encouraged to list various ways of getting what they want (for example, asking, hinting, and temper tantrums).   The children are then expected to catagorize the behaviors listed as either assertive, aggressive, or nonassertive.   Also early in the program children are helped to identify nonverbal behaviors that may be interpreted as either assertive, aggressive, or nonassertive.   In later sessions children have a chance to practice assertive behaviors, to work on thought processes that contribute to increased assertiveness, and to evaluate their personal progress toward increased assertiveness.   According to Rashbaum-Selig, this program has been used to help fifth and sixth graders to overcome such difficulties as shyness, uncontrollable temper, lack of initiative, and boredom.   She believes further that this and similar assertion programs can be used to help children come to terms with the changing sex roles in society.

In a related area, Downing (1977) has developed an approach for teaching children behavior change techniques.   This approach helps children to identify behaviors they value, to identify concerns about their own behavior, and to establish behavior change goals. In an experimental study, Downing found that children involved in his program made greater gains in academic achievement than did children in a control group as measured by the Peabody Individual Achievement Tests.   Differences in achievement were found in the areas of math, reading recognition, spelling, and general information and were significant at the .05 level of confidence. Downing also found that children who participated in his program attended school at a rate six percent higher than did children in the control group. Further, unlike children in the control group, children involved in the program improved their social behavior in the classroom according to teacher reports.

In general, then, many educational strategies and activities are available to facilitate children's development in the area of behavior. The multimodal educational framework suggests that teachers use a variety of these activities to help children develop and maintain new behaviors.

Affect

From the point of view of Lazarus (1973), "Every patient-therapist interaction involves ... 'affect' (be it the silent joy of nonjudgmental acceptance, or the sobbing release of pent-up anger)" (p. 406). Accordingly, multimodal education creates opportunities for elementary schoolchildren to experience time of nonjudgmental acceptance and release of feelings.

The Human Development Program (Bessell & Palomares, 1973) is an example of a program that allows children to express their feelings within a nonjudgmental environment. This program is widely known because it incorporates the "Magic Circle," a group activity lasting approximately 20 minutes that involves approximately 10 children in each session. During Magic Circle sessions, children are not required to share their feelings, but each child who does is assured either the leader or another participant will reflect the feeling expressed. Although the goals of the Magic Circle are varied, its main emphases are to help children become more aware of their feelings and to provide children with opportunities to express their feelings and respond to the feelings of others. Other programs, such as DUSO, attempt to achieve similar goals, but few other programs so obviously strive to create a nonjudgmental atmosphere in which children can express their feelings.

The Magic Circle is being used in many school districts and some studies have been conducted to assess its impact. In a school district in central Pennsylvania, elementary school teachers and counselors worked together to implement the Magic Circle program in virtually every elementary classroom in the district. Implementation was preceded by intensive training in small group leadership for both counselors and teachers. Included in this training were: (a) an introductory workshop that outlined the theory and practice of Magic Circles, (b) a handbook of objectives explaining, in part, the uses of the Magic Circle, and (c) opportunities for teachers and counselors to critique each other's leadership performance (Gerler, 1973).

After two years of the Magic Circle's use in this school system, Gerler and Pepperman (1976) conducted a follow-up study to assess if children viewed the Magic Circle as a place to openly express feelings without fear of reprisal and to determine whether children felt listened to during Magic Circle sessions. When asked, "Do other kids make fun of you when you talk in Magic Circles?" a large majority (72%) of the 400 children studied responded with a

"No." This response seems to indicate that most children perceive the Magic Circle as a safe place to express their feelings. At the same time, however, more study is obviously needed to determine why 28 percent of the children expressed some fear of reprisal for sharing their feelings in Magic Circles.

When asked, "Does the leader (teacher or counselor) listen to you when you talk in Magic Circles?" 94 percent of the children answered "Yes." On the other hand, when asked, "Do other kids listen to you when you talk in Magic Circles?" only about 43 percent of the children answered "Yes." The remainder answered with either a "No" or "Not sure." It appears, then that, while most children feel safe to share their feelings in Magic Circle sessions, many children are not sure their peers are interested enough to listen.

In general, even though much study remains to be done with the Magic Circle program, it appears to be a promising way to facilitate children's development in the affective domain.

Another procedure which is the best antidote for the affect of anxiety is relaxation training. Multimodal relaxation has been discussed in previous chapters. Such things as relaxation instructions or tapes (Keat, 1977) can be utilized with the entire class or placed in emotional resource centers (Keat, 1974a) where children can go when they feel uptight. These emotional resource centers can either be in the classroom (like a learning center) or in another room (such as the library). When children get hassled, they then have this back-up support to which they can go to relax by listening to the tapes with headphones or with an ear plug. If the training is to take place with the entire class, then a tape machine with clear audio and appropriate volume is needed. Some relaxation programs add in the dimension of sensory awareness. Rossman and Kahnweiler (1977), for example, have developed several relaxation exercises involving touching and listening which can be incorporated into a multimodal education program. In one exercise children are given the following instructions:

> Place one hand on your chest and one hand on your stomach feeling the movement of breath. Try breathing only into the stomach, then into the chest, feeling each rise and fall. Watch the changes in breathing and relax. Breathe through the nose. (p. 262)

In another exercise children are asked to do the following:

> Pay attention to your ears, their shape, make-up, muscles and temperature. Concentrate and listen to all sounds you can hear. Become aware of the number of sounds. Become aware of the different types of sounds. Slowly focus on the sounds inside of your head, letting them fill it peacefully. (p. 262)

By utilization of such programs as the human development one and procedures like relaxation training, the emotional life of children can be positively influenced.

Sensation

Children's lives are enriched by a multidisciplinary approach to the senses. Art teachers, for instance, deal with both visual and tactile stimuli by having children use fingerpaints to portray their feelings. Similarly, music teachers can select music that not only produces cognitive gains (e.g., Multiplication Rock, Capitol Records SJA-11174), but also teaches affective lessons (e.g., "Keep a happy outlook and be good to your friends" from "Lucky Seven Sampson" on Multiplication Rock).

The Centennial Schools of Lehigh University in Bethlehem, Pennsylvania have initiated an art program which helps children to better understand and use their senses (Evans & Gilmartin, 1976).   These schools accommodate children from six to 18 years of age who have been referred either because they are socially and emotionally disturbed or because their parents want them to have a unique educational experience. Recently, these schools hired a part-time art consultant to provide art shows for all students. This program in no way attempts to inculcate the aesthetic values of adults, but instead helps children to develop their own values through the use of their senses. According to Evans and Gilmartin (1976),

> The shows have inspired a number of creative and educational moments in the schools. The students not only look with their eyes, but often pass their hands over an art work. A sensuous marble torso had to be scrubbed every week to remove sticky fingerprints. (p. 274)

Another way to meet the sensory needs of children is by incorporating biofeedback activities into elementary school health education courses. Through biofeedback training, children can learn to control certain bodily processes in order to cultivate pleasurable sensations.   Some feedback training, for instance, can help individuals approach states of reverie comparable to those states achieved by persons during periods of high creativity (Danskin & Walters, 1973).

Kater and Spires (1975) have used biofeedback techniques to help children become aware of sensations which are not commonly noticed or discussed. Specifically, Kater and Spires have taught children in grades one to six to raise the temperature of their hands. These authors report that of the 167 children involved in this training 89 percent could raise the temperature of their hands within five minutes.   This kind of training not only helps to increase children's sensory awareness, but also can help children to "understand that their bodies are an important means of communication and that feelings are expressed through the body, even when they may not be consciously aware of it" (Kater & Spires, 1975, p.19).

In summary, whether through music, art, or biofeedback training, enhancing children's sensory awareness should be a major concern of the elementary school.   Accordingly, a multimodal curriculum incorporates activities to help children use all their senses more effectively.

Imagery

Another important aspect of multimodal education is to help children cultivate their mental images. Mental imagery is a central part of human functioning and therefore children's ability to work effectively in school may be determined in part by their ability to understand and manipulate mental images. Children's creativity, for instance, is affected to some degree by mental imagery. As Walkup (1965) has pointed out, creative persons seem able both to cultivate useful mental images and to manipulate these images in unusual ways. Similarly, Kelly (1974) has noted that relaxed states of mental imagery may increase the creative energies of some individuals.

Multimodal education strives to show children the interrelations of behavior, feelings, and mental imagery. One way to demonstrate the interrelations of these processes is through the use of the previously discussed relaxation exercises in the classroom. In relaxation exercises children not only practice deep breathing and isometric activities to achieve relaxation (Keat,1974b),but they also attempt to form mental images that lead to a relaxed state. For example, Koeppen (1974) describes how elementary school teachers and counselors can help children relax by employing the image of a baby elephant:

Hey! Here comes a cute baby elephant. But he's not watching where he's going. He doesn't see you lying there in the grass, and he's about to step on your stomach. Don't move. You don't have time to get out of the way. Just get ready for him. Make your stomach very hard. Tighten up your stomach muscles real tight. Hold it. It looks like he is going the other way. You can relax now. (p. 19)

Some children can also relax if they are encouraged to reflect on calm scenes or pleasant personal memories. Rossman and Kahnweiler (1977), for instance, ask children to imagine themselves on a beach just after a swim, moving their toes through the warm grains of sand on the beach. These authors also suggest that children imagine themselves walking through a large forest and then coming to a clearing. In the clearing is a person waiting with a gift which brings calm and relaxation. By experiencing such exercises, children may begin to grasp the interplay of calm behavior, peaceful feelings, and mental imagery.

Self-image, of course, is at the core of our very being. Children need to internalize the image that I am Loveable and Capable (IALAC) (Simon, 1973). In this procedure children can be read the story (Simon, 1973). Then they can draw their own IALAC signs. The class can discuss how the signs get torn away as the day progresses as well as develop strategies to deal with stresses which eat away at one's self-concept. For details about this exercise and 99 other ways to enhance self-concept, the interested reader is referred to an excellent book by Canfield and Wells (1976). Appendix F presents a self-image exercise.

Work in the imagery mode illustrates the interactive nature of the modes. By learning to develop pleasant scenes in your mind's eye, you enable yourself to feel more relaxed and thus less tense. A less hassled person generally has a more positive self-image because he/she then feels more competent and capable of coping with life's stresses.

Cognition

Some educators believe that this domain of the elementary school curriculum has received more than its share of attention in the past. Although this belief can probably be supported, there are certain cognitive areas that have received little attention. Most elementary schools provide few opportunities for children to consider the insights, philosophies, and judgments that constitute their fundamental values, attitudes, and beliefs even though many structured activities are available to help in this area.

One such activity is called "Twenty Things You Love To Do" (Simon, Howe, & Kirschenbaum, 1972) and is particularly enjoyable and instructive for children in the upper elementary grades. In this activity students are asked to list, as fast as they can, 20 things they enjoy doing. After making the list, students are asked to code their list as follows: (a) place a $ sign beside each item on the list which costs more than three dollars each time it is done; (b) place a "P" next to each item that is more fun to do with people and an "A" next to items which are more fun to do alone; (c) write the letters "PL" next to items that require planning; (d) write the code "N5" next to items that would not have been on the list five years ago; (e) place an "R" next to any item that requires either physical or emotional risk; (f) star the five items you most love to do; and (g) try to record by each item the date you last did it. The process of making and coding this list seems to help children recognize what activities they value most in life. An insight which might be gained is that although the student enjoys doing something (e.g., swimming), he or she hasn't done it for months. Therefore, they decide to go out and do it as soon as possible.

Schools also have not devoted much time to helping children consider the reasoning processes that go into the development of moral judgment. In this vein, Kohlberg's research has shown that children progress systematically through stages of moral development and that school programs which "systematically encourage students to examine the adequacy of their processes of reasoning and judgment have the effect of stimulating the development of higher stages of moral judgment" (Graham, 1975, p. 300). Facilitating children's development through the moral education processes advocated by Kohlberg and Turiel (1971) is an important aspect of the multimodal curriculum.

In addition to encouraging children to examine the reasoning processes that go into moral judgments, a multimodal curriculum can encourage children to reflect on their attitudes and beliefs about important subjects, such as death and divorce, which traditionally have had limited space in the elementary school curriculum. Clay (1976) recommends that children be given an understanding of the rituals surrounding death. He specifically suggests that they be provided with opportunities to play at having funerals, including such activities as putting a play figure into a box, putting the box into the ground, covering the box, having a brief ceremony, marking the grave with an appropriate symbol, and placing flowers on the grave. Stanford (1977) suggests that death education be made part of social studies classes, language arts classes, home economics classes, music classes, and art classes. He has devised some classroom activities to help children think about death. He recommends, for example, that students be asked to write a few paragraphs describing what they would like death to be like and why. Further, he suggests that students work in small groups to write a few original jokes about death and then discuss why people often choose to laugh about death.

Another area of relatively recent interest is that of divorce education. Indeed, with over one-third of our marriages resulting in divorce, almost every child's life will be affected by this happening either directly or through contact with friends whose parents are divorced. This topic can either be the basis for children of divorce groups (Wilkinson & Bleck, 1977) or a classroom topic. Materials which can be meaningfully used in the classroom are bibliotherapy (Gardner, 1970), tapes (Gardner, 1975), T. V.'s Inside/Out series ("Breakup"), or filmstrips (e.g., Guidance Associates, 1973).

The cognitive domain has received much attention in the elementary school classroom, but topics such as values clarification, moral education, death and divorce education are only beginning to find a place in the classroom. These topics may lead to some controversy between educators and parents. The multimodal framework suggests the need for elementary school personnel to examine unexplored areas in the cognitive domain for possible inclusion in the curriculum.

Interpersonal relations

Both DUSO and Magic Circle activities exemplify curricular programs that offer children opportunities to think about and practice their inter-actions with others. Similarly, transactional analysis (TA) activities (Berne, 1964) can be incorporated into elementary school social studies programs to offer children opportunities to conceptualize and role play social interactions. Children have fun with TA terms such as "strokes," "warm fuzzies," "cold prickles," "frozzies," and "prinzes" (Freed, 1973) and at the same time they can learn to examine the serious implications of interacting with people.

In addition to these commercially packaged curricular programs, many worthwhile activities have been developed for use on a smaller scale. The following activities can be considered under the friendship training rubric which was discussed earlier in this book. Myrick and Moni (1972), for instance, recommend an activity called "The Friendship Flag," which is designed to help children symbolize their ideas and feelings about friends and friendship. The only materials needed for this activity are a few samples of popular symbols that children will easily recognize, such as an American flag or a dollar sign, some drawing paper which contains a dittoed outline of a flag, and some pencils and crayons. The procedure is simple. The children participate in a brief discussion about the meaning and usefulness of certain symbols and then are asked to draw a flag to portray their ideas about friendship. Sometimes the flag can be partitioned into several sections with each section symbolizing a specific aspect of friendship. Myrick and Moni suggest that students symbolize each of the following on separate parts of the flag: (a) an occasion when someone was friendly to you; (b) an occasion when someone was unfriendly to you; (c) things you look for when choosing a friend; (d) something about you that appeals to others; and (e) something you would like to give a friend.

Similarly, Gumaer (1976b) has designed a classroom activity called "The Friendship Class." This activity consists of approximately 10 sessions in which children are given the chance to get to know each other better. In one session children are invited to share a secret about themselves with other class members. In other sessions children are invited to do such things as write a friendly letter to a classmate or to pair up with someone and talk about hobbies.

A program known as "Children's World Friendship" has been developed in Holland and Belgium to enhance children's interpersonal relations on a world-wide basis (Fasting, 1975). In this program, elementary school teachers are invited to have their classes exchange letters and art work with classes in other countries. These letters are sent to the offices of Children's World Friendship in The Hague where volunteers translate the letters. This program gives children personal ties with individuals from other cultures. The following excerpt from one of the letters illustrates the impact of the program:

> Now you like to know something of my family. I wrote you I am Togo boy. My father has 4 wives and my mother is the second wife. In all my family we are 7 boys and 8 good girls. My sisters love me and they give me things. I am so glad to be your friend here. (Fasting, 1975, p. 100).

It may be that personal contacts of this type are a step to the kind of understanding and friendship which will prevent the spread of racial and international tensions. This program could surely add variety and depth to the interpersonal aspects of multimodal education.

Drugs and Diet

Finally, the multimodal framework suggests that elementary schools help children understand the effects of drugs and diet on their lives, particularly on their behavior and emotions.

It is difficult to deny the importance of educational programs in the drug and alcohol area. Drugs and alcohol affect millions of lives. The National Commission on Marihuana and Drug Abuse (1973) reported that at least 14 percent of the 12- to 17-year-olds in the United States have experimented with marihuana for recreational and nonmedical purposes. According to Gade and Goodman (1975), "There are approximately eight million alcoholics in the

United States and they in turn influence another twenty-four million Americans who are members of their families" (p. 46).

To partially meet the need for drug education programs, Strandmark (1973) has recommended teaching strategies that take into account the flowing together of the affective and cognitive domains of the learner. He suggests three types of strategies. The first creates a separate course for drug education - a course that emphasizes self-understanding, human needs, perception, self-concept, and coping. A second approach incorporates confluent drug education into existing school courses such as social studies and health education. A third approach involves a community-wide drug education effort because school programs have little effect unless students receive support outside the school. Whatever approach to drug education is adopted, it is an important part of multimodal curriculum.

A second area of concern in the "D" zone of the BASIC ID is that of Diet (Keat, 1976c). Here the multidisciplinary forces in the school, represented by the nurse, teachers, administrators, counselors, psychologists, and physical education instructors, should work together to acquaint children with a sound approach to food selection. Children should become aware of the importance of eating certain foods (Fredericks, 1976) as well as avoiding others such as sugar-infested ones (Yudkin, 1972). In addition, elementary school personnel can collaborate to help children see the interrelations of physical exercise, sleep patterns, and nutrition as components of their life skills education. A variety of persons, including many outside the school (such as physicians and dieticians) can be brought into the regular classroom to assist with this kind of instruction.

CONCLUSION

The "BASIC ID framework of multimodal education provides elementary school personnel with a means for expanding their instructional offerings. The model has already been suggested for use in expanding career education offerings (Gerler, 1977). By using the BASIC ID as a guide, persons working in the schools can identify neglected instructional areas, implement class-room activities to correct the deficiencies, and increase their impact on the lives of children. It is only by using such a multimodal approach that we can hope to educate the whole child.

11 Multimodal Therapy: Getting It All Together

You have now been through a journey which has encompassed the broad spectrum approach of multimodal therapy with children. In the process you have been confronted with many tables which summarized the cogent points of the particular cases presented. The seven topical areas which follow represent an attempt to summarize, with a separate section for each modality of the BASIC ID, the problem areas and treatment techniques on a broader scale. Where appropriate, the interested reader is referred to specific pages in seven key references, (i.e., Blackham & Silberman, 1975; Lazarus, 1971, 1976; Keat, 1974a; Krumboltz & Thoresen, 1969, 1976 and Rimm & Masters, 1974) or to other selected resources. Multimodal Behavior Therapy (Lazarus, 1976) is an especially important reference and recommended as providing a foundation for the "catalogue" presented here. Wherever the Keat (1974a) and Rimm and Masters (1974) sources are cited, these years (i.e., 1974) are to be assumed.

Keat initiated this summary table several years ago and laid the foundation for this development. Since that time, several therapy procedures classes have provided input for the table. The current presentation represents a third revision and updating of the table and is primarily a result of the effort of Judah. As can be seen from this, the table is in a state of constant evolution and the authors challenge you to go on developing the table to suit your personalized needs.

As can be noted, there are several techniques that recur. For some of these often-cited procedures, appendices are presented for your further consideration. The following procedures are presented in appendices: anxiety management training (Appendix G), imagery treatment (Appendix H), cognitive therapy procedures (Appendix I), and interpersonal treatment ideas (Appendix J).

This summary table is not meant to be used as a cookbook without clinical

---

*This chapter was co-authored by Richard D. Judah.

intuition and compassion.   A constructive working relationship with your client is the usually necessary (but not sufficient) condition. This table should help you go beyond the relationship and get into effective procedures which can be sufficient for positive change.   A possible approach could be as follows: When you are confronted with a problem in your practice with which you are having difficulty, then you can consult the table (e.g., in the Behavior mode, "overtalking").   Next, look up the cited procedure(s) in the sources (e.g., Keat, 1974a, p. 82).   After reading about the approach and gaining a working understanding of the technique, if you feel you can carry out the procedure effectively, fine.   If not, then you may want to consult with a colleague or look for some supervision with the procedure.   In certain instances you may want to behaviorally rehearse the procedure with a friend or colleague.   Then you should be ready to give it a go with your client. By using your basic clinical skills along with the newly acquired procedures, you can help your client(s) more effectively.

These tables represent a start for the clinician to catalogue and develop techniques (i.e., "technical eclecticism," Lazarus, 1967) which are effective with different problem areas. The problems presented under each mode are alphabetized. Using this table as a focal point, you can add problem areas and treatment strategies and thus develop a comprehensive cookbook personalized to your own particular clinical practice.   The stance taken herein is that you are only limited by what you know and can do. As a professional you might take one technique a week (or one each month), read about it, share it with your staff, behaviorally rehearse it, and then try it out in your practice. In such a fashion you can add to your armamentarium of useful procedures and therefore continue to grow professionally.

Table 11-1
Behavior

Problem Area(s)	Treatment Procedure(s)
Acting out (e.g., fighting)	Behavior contracting (Keat, 78-82) Play therapy (Keat, 138) Point system (Sulzer & Mayer, 1972, 32-36) Systematic exclusion (Krumboltz & Thoresen, 1969, 89-132; Sulzer & Mayer, 1972, 170) Bibliotherapy (Keat, 112-113) Puppet play (Keat, 192-193) Directed Muscular Activity - DMA (Keat, 68; Lazarus, 1971, 98, 108-111) Instant Replay (Bedford, 1974) Timeout (Keat, 171-172; Patterson & Gullion, 1968, 56; Sulzer & Mayer, 1972, 154-161)

Problem Area(s)	Treatment Procedure(s)
Acting out (continued)	Mediating response (Lazarus, 1971, 208-209) Behavioral rehearsal (Blackham & Silberman, 1975, 213-224)
Appearance (poor grooming and dress)	Appearance training modules (Krumboltz & Thoresen, 1976, 517-527) Modeling (Krumboltz & Thoresen, 1969, 163-264) Before-after picture technique (Krumboltz & Thoresen, 1969, 424-425) Bibliotherapy (Keat, 111-112)
Behavior undesirable or unacceptable (excessive drinking, drug taking, overeating, smoking)	Behavior modification (Thoresen & Mahoney, 1974, 120-122; Yates, 1970, 305-319) Aversion therapy (Lazarus, 1971, 234) Multimodal behavior therapy (Lazarus, 1976, 116-132)
Behavioral deficits	Modeling (Krumboltz & Thoresen, 1969, 163-264)
Behavioral disorders (e.g., self-control, etc.)	Behavioral contract (Keat, 78-82; Krumboltz & Thoresen, 1976, 109-110) Bibliotherapy (Keat, 112,113) Timeout (Keat, 82-83, 171-172) Bathroom technique (Keat, 82) General behavioral strategies (Blackham & Silberman, 1975, 141-280) Homework assignments (Ellis & Harper, 1975, 205-206)
Bizarre talk	Selective reinforcement (Blackham & Silberman, 1975, 207-208)
Bullying	Give added responsibilities (Dreikurs, 1968, 94)
Criticism (unwarranted or excessive)	Positive expressiveness training (Lazarus, 1971, 234)

Problem Area(s)	Treatment Procedure(s)
Crying	Nonreinforcement (Blackham & Silberman, 1975, 65-66) Successive approximation (Keat, 167-168) Revising contingencies (Yates, 1970, 353-354)
Defiance	Logical consequences (Dinkmeyer & McKay, 1973, 108-113) Contracting (Keat, 78-82)
Disobedience	Conditioning strategies (Blackham & Silberman, 1975, 36-39, 272-274)
Delinquency	Assertive training (Rimm &Masters, 121) Contingency management (Rimm & Masters, 250-261) Covert sensitization (Rimm & Masters, 390) Modeling (Krumboltz & Thoresen, 1976, 57-67, Rimm & Masters, 135) Shaping (Rimm & Masters, 189) Differential reinforcement (Wolpe & Lazarus, 1966, 210) Live-in programs (Blackham & Silberman, 1975,164-166)
Demanding behavior	Contingency reinforcement (Blackham & Silberman, 1975, 252-254)
Depression	Catalogue of rewarding activities (Keat, 322-325) Graded exercises (Lazarus, 1971, 112-113)
Echolalia	Modeling (Rimm & Masters, 133) Differential reinforcement (Bandura, 1969, 156)
Enuresis, Encopresis	Behavioral contracts (Haley, 1973, 66-68, 169-171, 176-178; Yates, 1970, 98) Alarm apparatus (Lazarus, 1971, 213-214) Multiple techniques (Krumboltz & Thoresen, 1976, 214-220)

Problem Area(s)	Treatment Procedure(s)
Enuresis, Encopresis (Continued)	Systematic reinforcement (Blackham & Silberman, 1975, 208-212; Krumboltz & Thoresen, 1976, 221-234)
Exhibitionism	Aversive counterconditioning (Bandura, 1969, 318, 520) Desensitization (Bandura, 1969, 466-477; Blackham & Silberman, 1975, 78-79)
Fetishism	Aversive counterconditioning (Bandura, 1969, 337-338; 523-524)
Gambling	Environmental consequences (Krumboltz &Thoresen, 1976, 138-143) Aversion therapy (Yates, 1970, 347-348)
Habits (maladaptive)	Counterconditioning (Lazarus, 1971, 210) R.I.D. (Recognize, Imitate: negative practice, Drop) (in Lazarus, 1972, 165)
Head banging	Massed practice (Yates, 1970, 354) Aversion therapy (Blackham & Silberman, 1975, 73-74)
Hoarding	Satiation (Kazdin, 1975, 108)
Hyperactivity	Aversion relief therapy (Lazarus, 1971, 157-158) Drug treatment (Wolpe & Lazarus, 1966, 120) Diet (Feingold, 1975) Environmental structuring (Keat, 233-241) Modeling (Keat, 73-74; 115-118;) (Krumboltz & Thoresen, 1969, 207-210;) (Sulzer & Mayer, 1972, 149-150) DMA Behavioral contracts Timeout Relaxation exercises Study booth

Problem Area(s)	Treatment Procedure(s)
Hyperactivity (Continued)	Differential reinforcement (Ross, 1974, 282-283) Stimulus control (Krumboltz & Thoresen, 1969, 30-33; Sulzer & Mayer, 1972, 133) Aversive conditioning (Rimm & Masters, 380-381) Positive reinforcement schedule (Krumboltz & Thoresen, 1969, 30-33)
Inhibitions (excessive)	Exaggerated role taking (Lazarus, 1971, 233) Assertiveness training (Lazarus, 1971, 115-127)
Interviewing skills, poor	Behavioral rehearsal (Krumboltz & Thoresen, 1969, 414-428)
Littering	Incentive system (Kazdin, 1975)
Loitering	Developing alternative behaviors (Krumboltz & Krumboltz, 1972, 171-172)
Lying	Extinction (Sulzer & Mayer, 1972, 133) Blow up (Lazarus, 1971, 230) Differential reinforcement (Blackham & Silberman, 1975, 278-279)
Nail biting	Behavioral contracting (Rimm & Masters, 284-287)
Obscene behavior and talk	Timeout (Keat, 82-83, 171-172) Response cost (Blackham & Silberman, 1975, 178)
Overtalking	Timeout (Keat, 82) Peer pressure (Ackerman, 1972, 103) Team effort (Blackham & Silberman, 1971, 141) Peer models (Blackham & Silberman, 1971, 141) Self-control techniques (Blackham & Silberman, 1975, 237-238)

Problem Area(s)	Treatment Procedure(s)
Procrastination	Contingency management (Keat, 165-169) Reinforcement menu (Krumboltz & Thoresen, 1969, 42-45) Verbal commitment to goal (Krumboltz & Thoresen, 1969, 55)
Quietness	Internalization of anticipatory consequences (Bandura, 1969, 617-618)
Resistance to counseling	Inner circle strategy (Keat, 145-146; Lazarus, 1971, 81-87) Role reversal (Rimm & Masters, 95-98)
Self-induced seisures	Contingency management (Rimm & Masters, 199)
Self-injury	Assertive training (Rimm & Masters, 115) Aversion control (Blackham & Silberman, 1975, 73-74; Rimm & Masters, 379-380) Covert sensitization (Rimm & Masters, 398) Contingency management (Rimm & Masters, 198) Aversive consequences (Bandura, 1969, 513; Kazdin, 1975, 148-149)
Sleeping difficulty	Relaxation training (Keat, 68; Keat, 1977; Lazarus, 1975) Stimulus control (Kazdin, 1975, 196)
Sloppiness	Saturday Box (Blackham & Silberman, 1975, 260-261) Appearance training modules (Krumboltz & Thoresen, 1976, 517-527) Modeling (Krumboltz & Thoresen, 1969, 163-264)
Stealing	Contract (Keat, 78-82) Restitution (Keat, 83) Negative reinforcement (Keat, 82)

Problem Area(s)	Treatment Procedure(s)
Stealing (Continued)	Response cost (Blackham & Silberman, 1975, 277-278) Positive reinforcement (Blackham & Silberman, 1975, 277-278)
Sulking	Differential reinforcement (Krumboltz & Krumboltz, 1972, 11-12)
Tantrum	Bathroom technique (Dreikurs & Soltz, 1964, 158; Keat, 82) Extinction (Blackham & Silberman, 1975, 65-66) Timeout (Keat, 82-83, 171-172) The "turtle" technique (Krumboltz & Thoresen, 1976, 157-162)
Tardiness	Behavioral contracts (Krumboltz & Thoresen, 1976, 109-110) Systematic exclusion (Krumboltz & Thoresen, 1969, 114) Token reinforcers (Blackham & Silberman, 1975, 174-175; Krumboltz & Thoresen, 1969, 135-136)
Tattling	Extinction (Blackham & Silberman, 1975, 64-68; Keat, 82-83)
Thumbsucking	Cueing and modeling (Krumboltz & Krumboltz, 1972, 82-83)
Time: Unconstructive use of it	Model reinforcement treatment (Krumboltz & Thoresen, 1969, 234-241)
Unemployment (chronic)	"POUNCE" technique (Krumboltz & Thoresen, 1969, 399-414)
Word mumbling	Verbal projection exercises
Withdrawal and nonassertive behavior	Assertive training (Alberti & Emmons, 1974; Keat, 70-71; Krumboltz & Thoresen, 1976, 29-36, 475-486; Lazarus, 117-127 (1971), 155-157) Rehearsal desensitization (Lazarus, 1971, 128-130)

Problem Area(s)	Treatment Procedure(s)
Withdrawal and nonassertive behavior (Continued)'	Group confrontation Differential reinforcement (Bandura, 1969, 26-27)

AFFECT

Aggression	Aversive counterconditioning (Bandura, 1969, 527) Cognitive restructuring (Bandura, 1969, 382-383) Differential reinforcement (Bandura, 1969, 106-110) Modeling (Bandura, 1969, 128-129, 159-161) Reinforcement withdrawal (Bandura, 1969, 343-345, 384-385) Assertive training (Rimm & Masters, 105-108) Contingency management (Rimm & Masters, 198) Interaction restructuring (Krumboltz & Thoresen, 1976, 174-179) Home and school-based reinforcement (Krumboltz & Thoresen, 1969, 130-188) Contracting (Blackham & Silberman, 1975, 220-221)
Aloneness, shyness	Relationship training (Keat, 60) Activities (Keat, 87) Behavioral rehearsal (Keat, 71-73) Assertiveness training (Krumboltz & Thoresen, 1976, 29-35) Modeling (Blackham & Silberman, 1975, 212-214)
Anger expression	"Hostile Pillow" (Keat, 196) Puppet play (Keat,192-193) Gestalt techniques (Perls, 1969, 76-81)
Anger, lack of self-control	Imaginal aversive contingency (Krumboltz & Thoresen, 1969, 319-327)

Problem Area(s)	Treatment Procedure(s)
Anxiety	Relaxation training (Goldfried & Davison, 1976, 81-111; Keat, 67-68; Krumboltz & Thoresen, 1969, 312-313; Lazarus, 1970; Lazarus, 1971, 273-275) Flooding (Lazarus, 1971, 109-110, 230-232) Transcendental meditation (Ornstein, 1972, 104-140) Contact desensitization (Krumboltz & Thoresen, 1969, 168-178) Cue control Systematic desensitization (Krumboltz & Thoresen, 1976, 269-279) Anxiety-Management training (Lazarus, 1976, 103-115)
Blocked feelings	Directed muscular activity (DMA: Keat, 68, 75; Lazarus, 1971, 108-111) Talking, Feeling, Doing Game (Gardner, 1973) Bag of words game (Gardner, 1975, 307-323) Inner circle strategy Role playing (Rimm & Masters, 86-87)
Block feelings (lack of expression of feeling)	Positive and negative expressions (Lazarus, 1971, 135-140) Encapsulated personalities (Lazarus, 1971, 130-132) Bibliotherapy (Alberti & Emmons, 1974) Board of Objects Game (Gardner, 1975, 227-262) Talking, feeling, doing game (Gardner, 1973)
Depression	Multimodal behavior therapy (Lazarus, 1976, 97-101)
Face-saving	Anxiety relief procedure (Lazarus, 1971, 221)
Fears, panic attacks, phobias	Systematic desensitization (Keat, 68-70; Krumboltz & Thoresen, 1976, 269-279, 284-286; Lazarus, 1971, 96-111; Marquis, Morgan & Piaget, 1973)

Problem Area(s)	Treatment Procedure(s)
Fears, panic attacks, phobias (Continued)	Flooding (Rimm & Masters, 339-342)
	Modeling (Rimm & Masters, 148-155)
	Thought stopping (Rimm & Masters, 438-442)
	Covert extinction (Rimm & Masters, 322-325)
	Paradoxical intentions (Lazarus, 1971, 232; Haley, 1973)
	Participant modeling and self-directed practice (Krumboltz & Thoresen, 1976, 301-311)
	In-vivo emotive imagery (Krumboltz & Thoresen, 1976, 248-264, 316-319)
	Kung-fu training (Krumboltz & Thoresen, 1976, 312-315)
	Desensitization procedures (Blackham & Silberman, 1975, 195-200, 271-272)
Guilt	Rational emotive (Ellis & Harper, 1975; Keat, 75-77)
	Anticipatory consequences (Bandura, 1969, 617-618)
Joy (absence of enthusiasm and spontaneous feelings)	Positive imagery procedures (Lazarus, 1971, 209, 319-327)
	Anticipation processes (Lazarus, 1971, 184)
	Reinforcement survey schedule (Keat, Appendix D); Chapter 4 in this book.
Suicidal feelings (depression)	Positive self-sentences (Hauck, 1972 113-124)
	Time projection (Lazarus, 1971, 227-229)
	"As if" (Lazarus, 1971, 226-227)
	Self reinforcement (Thoresen & Mahoney, 1974, 11-85)
	Rewarding activities (Keat, 87)

SENSATION-SCHOOL

Adult (Sensation)	
Back (lower) pains	Orthopedic exercises

Problem Area(s)	Treatment Procedure(s)
Blindness	Mobility training (Hardy & Cull, 1972, 213-264) Career counseling (Hardy & Cull, 1972, 275-334) Rehabilitation teaching Seeing-eye dog
Colitis	Multimodal (Lazarus, 1976, 160-169)
Frigidity	Aversion relief therapy (Lazarus, 1971, 157-159) Sexual reeducation (Krumboltz & Thoresen, 1976, 83-88)
Headaches	Muscle relaxation training Krumboltz & Thoresen, 1976, 344-348; Tasto & Hinkle, 1973, 347-349)
Heart troubles	Cardiac stress management training (CSMT) (Krumboltz & Thoresen, 1976, 349-359)
Inner tremors	Gendlin's focusing methods (Lazarus, 1971, 232)
Insomnia	Stimulus control and progressive relaxation (Krumboltz & Thoresen, 1976, 328-343)
Muscle tone	Behavioral exercise programming (Krumboltz & Thoresen, 1976, 349-359) Aerobics (Cooper, 1968)
Premature ejaculation	Training in increase threshold of excitability (Lazarus, 1971, 159-160) "Squeeze Technique" (Lazarus, 1971, 160-161)
Sensory awareness, low degree of	Experiential focusing technique (Lazarus, 1971, 232-233)
Sensual pleasure lacking	Sensate focus (Masters & Johnson, 1970, 67-91)

Problem Area(s)	Treatment Procedure(s)
Sexual inadequacy	Graded sexual assignments (Lazarus, 1971, 151-153) Sexual reeducation (Krumboltz & Thoresen, 1976, 83-88)
Stomach spasms	Breathing exercises (Keat, 67-68)
Tensions in jaw and neck	Differential relaxation
Tics	Massed practice (Rimm & Masters, 325-330) Habit reversal (Azrin & Nunn, 1973, 619-628)

Child: (School)

Academic success, poor perception of	Develop an "experience table" (Krumboltz & Thoresen, 1969, 333)
Accident prone	Motor coordination training (Keat, 74-75) Visuo-Motor behavior rehearsal (Krumboltz & Thoresen, 1976, 360-366)
Autocratic classroom	Classroom meetings (Glasser, 1969; Keat, 151-156)
Career decision making (poor perception of consequences)	Game therapy (Krumboltz & Thoresen, 1969, 308-316)
Class clown	Timeout (Keat, 82-83)
Classroom behaviors (disruptive)	Systematic exclusion (Krumboltz & Thoresen, 1969, 89-129) Self-monitoring (Mahoney, 1974) Timeout (Keat, 82-83) Token economy (Blackham & Silberman, 1975, 152-160) Classroom management procedures (Blackham & Silberman, 1975, 168-190)
Classroom participation, poor	Filmed social modeling (Krumboltz & Thoresen, 1969, 202-207)

Problem Area(s)	Treatment Procedure(s)
Classroom problems	Group sessions with children of similar problems (Dreikurs, 1968, 197)
Classroom productivity, low	Token reinforcement (Krumboltz & Thoresen, 1969, 133-139) Self-controlled reinforcement schedule (Mahoney & Thoresen, 1974, 111-128)
Fear of speaking in group	Role playing (Krumboltz & Thoresen, 1976, 360-361) Social modeling (Krumboltz & Thoresen, 1969, 202-207, 234-241) Systematic desensitization (Krumboltz & Thoresen, 1976, 265-268)
Handwriting, poor	Program (Skinner & Krakower, 1968)
Motivation (lack of)	Behavioral contracts (Keat, 78-82) Card carriers (Krumboltz & Thoresen, 1969, 142-150)
Perceptual-motor problems	Perceptual training programs (Frostig, 1966)
Phobia	Systematic desensitization (Keat, 69) Rewards contingent upon going to school (Madsen & Madsen, 1972, 67-68) Emotive imagery (Krumboltz & Thoresen, 1976, 316-319) Return the child to school immediately if the main reason is the mother's reinforcement of school avoidance (Keat et al., 1974, 66) Ignore bodily complaints. Make a doctor's appointment for after school, if thought necessary (Madsen & Madsen, 1972, 68) Modeling and self-directed practice (Krumboltz & Thoresen, 1976, 301-311) Family-counseling (Krumboltz & Thoresen, 1976, 280-288) Counterconditioning (Blackham & Silberman, 1975, 195-200, 271-272)

Problem Area(s)	Treatment Procedure(s)
Reading, poor	Tutoring Make relevant (Haley, 1973, 174-175)
School (interpersonal focus)	Affective education (Keat, 186-205; Keat et al., 1972) Communication skill training (Keat, 147-151, 152-159)
School difficulties	Restructuring environment (Keat, 165-173, 238-261; Keat et al., 1974, 1-8) Exaggerated role taking (Lazarus, 1971, 233)
Sensory expression	Dance (Kinesthetic: Ferreira, 1973, 95-115) Movement education (Keat et al., 1972) Music (Auditory: Keat, 124-126, 193-194; Bonny & Savary, 1973, 55-65, 66-89, 144-151) Art therapy (Kramer, 1971)
Speech difficulties	Speech therapy Scriptotherapy (Lazarus, 1976, 125-127) Aversive contingency system (Bandura, 1969, 327-328) Drawing pictures Successive approximation to alleviate elective silence (Blackham & Silberman, 1975, 200-204; Krumboltz & Thoresen, 1976, 89-97)
Study habits, poor	Recommend techniques for improved studying (Krumboltz & Thoresen, 1976, 454-467; Zifferblatt, 1970)
Studying difficulties	Time scheduling and reinforcement techniques (Krumboltz & Thoresen, 1969, 64-69, 471-485; 1976, 454-467) Time distortion (Haley, 1973, 116-123)
Stuttering	Fluency exercises (Lazarus, 1971, 219) Covert extinction (Rimm & Masters, 192-200) Negative practice (Rimm & Masters, 325-330)

Problem Area(s)	Treatment Procedure(s)
Test anxiety	Structured group interaction (Krumboltz & Thoresen, 1969, 471-485) Implosion (Cornish & Dilley, 1973, 499-503) Meditation (Akins & Nurnberg, 1976) Systematic desensitization (Blackham & Silberman, 1975, 230-232; Krumboltz & Thoresen, 1976, 269-279)
Time: Inefficient use of	Audio tape social modeling (Krumboltz & Thoresen, 1969, 234-240)
Truancy	Shaping and positive reinforcement (Lazarus, 1971, 210-211) Behavioral programming (Krumboltz & Thoresen, 1976, 47-55) Behavioral contracting (Krumboltz & Thoresen, 1969, 87) Modeling positive behaviors (Krumboltz & Thoresen, 1969, 163-166)
Vocational opportunities - Failure to explore	Simulation (Krumboltz & Thoresen, 1969, 293-306) Information-seeking skill building (Blackham & Silberman, 1975, 234-236)

IMAGERY

Adopted: Fears being left	Thought stopping (Lazarus, 1971, 229-231)
Ambivalence	Eidetic imagery (Lazarus, 1971, 226-227)
Anxieties	Desert island fantasy (Lazarus, 1971, 66-81)
Blocked feelings	Empty chair technique (Perls, 1969, 77-123)
Depression	Time projection (Lazarus, 1971, 228-229) Anticipation training (Krumboltz & Thoresen, 1976, 67-74)
Dreams about bombing	Eidetic imagery: Feelings of safeness (Lazarus, 1972, 87-99)
Emotionally upset (in general)	Negative imagery (Ellis & Harper, 1975, 210-213) Positive imagery (Ellis & Harper, 1975, 213-215)

Problem Area(s)	Treatment Procedure(s)
Excessive fantasy	Secondary reinforcement and modeling (Blackham & Silberman, 1975, 207)
Fears: Dentist, public speaking, etc.	"Emotive imagery" (Keat, 77, 296-297; Keat et al., 1974, 56-65; Krumboltz &Thoresen, 1976, 316-319; Lazarus, 1971, 211-212)
Funeral scenes	Desensitization (Wolpe, 1969)
Mother shouting "you fool"	"Empty chair" (Perls, 1969, e.g., 76-81, 83-89, 95-98, 141-146)
Nightmares	Systematic desensitization (Yates, 1970, 352)
Obsessive-compulsive	Rational imagery (Lazarus, 1971, 178-180) Positive imagery
Phobias (e.g., snakes, bugs)	Implosive therapy (Lazarus, 1971, 109-111)
Rebellious behavior	Aversive imagery (Lazarus, 1971, 208-209) "One-downsmanship" (Krumboltz & Thoresen, 1969, 319-327)
Rejection (fear of)	Implosion (Rimm & Masters, 333-348)
Roles, rigid	Exaggerated role-taking (Lazarus, 1971, 233)
Rumination over past	"As if" procedure (Lazarus, 1971, 226-227)
Self-confidence, lack of	Time projection (Lazarus, 1971, 227-229)
Self-image, low	Mutual storytelling (Keat, 84-86) Use of mirrors (Keat, 121-122) Incomplete sentences (Keat, 122-124)

COGNITION

Absolutistic thinking	Lessen "Musturbation" (Ellis & Harper, 1975, 202-205; Lazarus, 1976, 39-41)

Problem Area(s)	Treatment Procedure(s)
Absolutistic thinking (Continued)	Paradoxical therapy (Lazarus, 1976, 180-188)
Belief system, narrow	"After the Holocaust" (Lazarus, 1971, 174-196) Number-letter technique (Lazarus, 1971, 222-223) Cognitive restructuring (Lazarus, 1971, 167-168) Paradoxical therapy (Lazarus, 1976, 180-188)
Career information-seeking skills, lacking	Simulation (Krumboltz & Thoresen, 1969) Taped models (Krumboltz & Thoresen, 1969, 213-234) Experience-based career exploration (Krumboltz & Thoresen, 1976, 384-388)
Depression	Thought stopping (Lazarus, 1971, 229-231) Rewards for positive self-statements
Dichotomous reasoning in adolescents	Truth value technique (Lazarus, 1971, 167-168) Cognitive restructuring (Keat, 75-78)
Exaggerating future events	"So what if" (Lazarus, 1971, 222)
Goal formation	Structuring (Krumboltz & Thoresen, 1969, 52-58)
Guilt	"Two peach parable" (Lazarus, 1971, 172-174) Enculturation techniques (Lazarus, 1971, 171-176) "Shame" exercises (Ellis, 1972)
Irrational self-talk (e.g., failure, fears)	Deliberate rational disputation and corrective self talk (RET) (Ellis, 1962; Ellis & Harper, 1975; Keat, 75-77; Lazarus, 1971, 163-184; Lazarus & Fay, 1975; Dyer, 1976)
Memories (painful)	Systematic desensitization Relaxation plus rational assurance (Lazarus, 1971, 97)

Problem Area(s)	Treatment Procedures(s)
Misbehavior (chronic)	Imaginal aversive contingency (Krumboltz & Thoresen, 1969, 322-323)
Musturbation	Rational emotive therapy (Ellis, 1962, 60-88)
Overreaction to an event	Blow up (Lazarus, 1971, 230-232) Paradoxical therapy (Lazarus, 1976, 180-188)
Overgeneralization	Probability (Lazarus, 1971, 169)
Powerless in situation	"One Downsmanship" technique (Krumboltz & Thoresen, 1969, 323-324)
Problems making choices	Decision-making practice (Carkhuff, 1973, 91-134; Goldfried & Davison, 1976, 186-207; Gordon, 1974, 217-282; Keat, 150-156; Krumboltz & Thoresen, 1976, 368-414) Bibliotherapy (Bennett, 1963, 283-290) Token economy (Krumboltz & Thoresen, 1976, 377-378) Bibliotherapy (Krumboltz & Thoresen, 1976, 378-380)
Reliance (excessive) on other people's judgment	Training in differences between report and judgment (Lazarus, 1971, 169-170)
Sexual misinformation	Sex education (Bibliotherapy) (Keat, 78; Keat et al., 1974, 76-81) Sex reeducation (Krumboltz & Thoresen, 1976, 83-88)
Values	Clarification exercises (Simon et al., 1972) Games (e.g., "Careers," Keat, 193) "Blow up" technique (Lazarus, 1971, 230-232)

INTERPERSONAL RELATIONS

Autism (complete social withdrawal)	Token economy (Rimm & Masters, 218-248) Shaping procedures (Rimm & Masters, 187-189)

Problem Area(s)	Treatment Procedure(s)
Bullying	"No-lose method" (Gordon, 1970, 194-264) Classroom meeting (Glasser, 1969), 122-144) Modeling, role playing and behavioral rehearsal Mutual storytelling (Gardner, 1975)
Companionship (identify)	Buddy program (Keat, 255-256)
Conflict: Marital	Conjugal procedures (e.g., communication training) Contracts (Knox, 1971, 22-28; Patterson, 1971, 70-77) Breakdown of dichotomous reasoning (Lazarus, 1971, 167-168) Accelerative behavioral techniques (Krumboltz & Thoresen, 1976, 188-198) Constructive criticism training (Lazarus, 1971, 137-138) Positive expressiveness training (Lazarus, 1971, 138-139) Direct mutual communication (Ivey, 1971, 168-173) Behavioral rehearsal (Krumboltz & Thoresen, 1969, 436-437) Communication training (Krumboltz & Thoresen, 1976, 188-198) Fight therapy (Bach & Goldberg, 1974)
Conflict: with mother	Positive reinforced areas of child social interactions (Bandura, 1969, 375-377)
Conflicts: parent-child	"Family Council" (Dreikurs & Soltz, 1964) Family meeting (Dinkmeyer & McKay, 1973, 209-227) Parent education (Gordon, 1970; Krumboltz & Thoresen, 1976, 418-425; 434-444)
Dating anxiety (fear of approaching members of the opposite sex)	Behavioral rehearsal (Krumboltz & Thoresen, 1976, 36-46) Social modeling (Krumboltz & Thoresen, 1969, 435-436)

Problem Area(s)	Treatment Procedure(s)
Death	Bibliotherapy (e.g., Furman, 1974; Grollman, 1970)
Deficits	Behavior rehearsal (Keat, 71-73, 115-118; Lazarus, 1971, 123-127)
Depression	Social skill training (Lazarus, 1976, 100-101)
Divorce	Bibliotherapy (Gardner, 1970)
Exploited easily	Family therapy (Keat, 138-139; Lazarus, 1971, 212-214)
Fears group	Implosion (Lazarus, 1971, 109-111)
Filial relationships lacking	Filial therapy (Keat, 88, 138, 163)
Interpersonal problems	Multimodal group therapy (Lazarus, 1976, 149-159) Gaming methods (Sax & Hollander, 1972) Communication training (Keat, 147-159) Approximations of real-life situations (Krumboltz & Thoresen, 1969, 431-433)
Jealousy	Systematic desensitization (Marquis et al., 1973, 43)
Mistrust of people	Differential reinforcement (Krumboltz & Thoresen, 1969, 45-48)
Overdependence	Self-sufficiency assignments (Keat et al., 1974, 36) Parent training for raising a responsible child (e.g., Dinkmeyer & McKay, 1973) Reinforcement of successive approximation (Blackham & Silberman, 1975, 262-264)
Passivity, shyness	Assertive training (Blackham & Silberman, 1975, 189-190, 213-214; Krumboltz & Thoresen, 1976, 29-35; Rimm & Masters, 81-124) Behavioral rehearsal (Krumboltz & Thoresen, 1976, 25-36) Modeling (Rimm & Masters, 125-161)

Problem Area(s)	Treatment Procedure(s)
Peer interaction poor	Group therapy (Keat, 108-118; Lazarus, 1971, 187-193) Friendship training (Keat & Guerney, 1978) "Hot seat" (Keat, 260)
Poor communication skills	Modeling (Rimm & Masters, 1974, 130-138) Microtraining (Ivey, 1971, 106)
Prejudice	Group role playing (Bennett, 1963, 116-121)
Sharing	Solutions (Keat et al., 1974, 11)
Sibling rivalry	Bibliotherapy (e.g., "Instant Replay" Bedford, 1974) "As if" (Lazarus, 1971, 226) Differential reinforcement (Krumboltz & Krumboltz, 1972, 18-19)
Single parents (divorced, death)	Parents without partners Bibliotherapy (e.g., Grollman, 1970) Bibliotherapy (e.g., Gardner, 1970)
Suspicious (overly)	Exaggerated role taking (Lazarus, 1971, 233) Cognitive restructuring Positive expressiveness training Group inner-circle exercise
Timidity and embarrassment	Assertive training (Rimm & Masters, 93-105)

DRUGS-DIET

Activity and energy levels	Megavitamin therapy (Adams & Murray, 1973; Rosenberg & Feldzamen, 1974)
Alcoholism (or excessive drinking)	Change of beverage (needs glass in hand) Medication: to cause vomiting Aversion (Lazarus, 1971, 236; Thoresen & Mahoney, 1974, 26, 120-122) Alcoholics Anonymous Controlled intake (Krumboltz & Thoresen, 1976, 144-149)

Problem Area(s)	Treatment Procedure(s)
Anorexia nervosa	Systematic desensitization and reinforcement (Blackham & Silberman, 1975, 258-259)
Depression	Drug therapy (Lazarus, 1976, 65-85)
Hyperactivity, short attention span	Drug therapy (e.g., CNS stimulants for paradoxical effect with minimal brain dysfunction children)
Malnutrition or overweight	Diet therapy consultation (Stuart & Davis, 1972)
	Self-control techniques (Krumboltz & Thoresen, 1976, 106-116; Mahoney & Thoresen, 1974)
	Cognitive procedures (Krumboltz & Thoresen, 1976, 99-116)
	Multimodal behavior therapy (Lazarus, 1976, 170-179)
Manic and psychotic reactions	Drug therapy (Lazarus, 1976, 65-85)
Smoking and other drug abuses	Aversion (Lazarus, 1971, 234- 237)
	Drug education (Keat et al., 1974, 82-87)
	Self-control techniques (Mahoney& Thoresen, 1974, 218-246)
	Satiation (Blackham & Silberman, 1975, 233-234)
	Coverant control (Krumboltz & Thoresen, 1976, 117-123)
	"Broad-range" techniques (Krumboltz & Thoresen, 1976, 124-137)
	Selective reinforcement (Blackham & Silberman, 1975, 233-234)
	Covert sensitization (Blackham & Silberman, 1975, 233-234)

A Relaxation Directions for Children

1. <u>Breathing</u>: I want to teach you how to breathe. The first thing we'll do is have a kind of contest. Take a deep breath, just like you're going to do when you play trumpet, take a deep breath, and then see who can let it out for the longest time. Real slow, as slow as you can and while you're letting your breath out, make a sound like "Aaah", or "S", and let the air out real slow, and see how long you can keep it going. Take a real deep breath, as I raise my hand and when I start to bring it down, make a sound (Pause)...O.K.; when we learn how to play the trumpet, or run, we take a deep breath down here below the stomach. It can help you in doing all of these things. Now, take a deep breath, and breathe down here. O.K. let's try it again. Deep breath, down in guts. Let's go (Pause).... That's good! Let's practice this next week. It's helpful when you run or ride your bike, or swim, or play basketball. Notice how a guy before he takes a foul shot, takes a deep breath and blows it out, just before he shoots, and then he is really relaxed. Breathing away tension. Breathing is the key to relaxation. Okay take a deep breath and let out a sigh. A sigh of relief. Then you feel better--calm and cool. Use this whenever you feel uptight or tense.

2. <u>Muscles, Tension-Relaxation</u>: The first muscle I want to start with is your fist. With the fist, make believe you're going to squeeze an orange or a tennis ball, and squeeze as hard as you can for five seconds. O.K. let's go. Remember, as we count to 5 each time, at 3 begin taking in your deep breath. 1 ... 2 ... 3 ... 4 ... 5 O.K. let go of your breath. Shake hands to get juice off or like basketball players do to stay loose. Now let's do both hands; 1 ... 2 ... 3 ... 4 ... 5 ... (take your deep breath at 3, let it out at 5). Now let's make believe you're Superman, and make a big muscle like this (show how). Bend back your arm, 1 ... 2 ... 3 ... (breath) 4 ... 5 ... let go, shake loose. O.K. let's do both arms like Mr. America; 1 ... 2 ... 3 ... (breath) 4 ... 5 ... (let go). As you let go of your arms, also let out your breath. Shake loose. Now let's stretch, stand up and stretch toward the ceiling, reach as high as you can (like your getting right out of bed); O.K., now I'd like to work with some other muscles. Like make believe that you have a giant jawbreaker, and you're

going to bite it as hard as you can, for 5 seconds; 1 ... 2 ... 3 ... (breathe in) 4 ... 5 ... (breathe out). Relax now and let out your deep breath that you started taking in on three. Nice and slow and easy. Also, yawn as hard as you can. Stretch jaw open as far as you can. Now smile, like you're going to try to touch your ears with the corner of your mouth, 1 ... 2 ... 3 ... (breathe in) 4 ... 5 ... (breathe out). O.K. then relax. And take another deep breath. Now let's make believe that you have a fly that's coming around and lands on your nose. Wrinkle it up; 1 ... 2 ... 3 ... (breathe in) 4 ... 5 ... (breathe out). Oh, there he goes; he flew away. Let go and relax. Next, you know how a turtle pulls in his head when he's scared of something. O.K. you pull in your head like into a shell, as hard as you can. Pull in your neck like into the turtle shell. 1 ... 2 ... 3 ... (in) 4 ... 5 ... (out). Relax, move around; roll your neck around, and get it nice and loose.

What I'd like you to do for your shoulders is to have you shrug your shoulders as high as you can; 1 ... 2 ... 3 ... (in) 4 ... 5 ... (out). O.K. let it go as you let go of your breath.

Now arch your back. Sit-up, as straight as you can; 1 ... 2 ... 3 ... (in) 4 ... 5 ... (out). Relax back into the way you were.

Now to do something for your stomach. Make believe I'm going to punch you in the stomach. What would you do? Make your muscles real tight? I would. Make it hard. Here goes 1 ... 2 ... 3 ... (in) 4 ... 5 ... (out) let go; breath out and let your stomach relax. Now I want to show you a couple of things for your legs, for the different muscles of your legs. Push your heels down as hard as you can; 1 ... 2 ... 3 ... (in) 4 ... 5 ... (out) let go. O.K. the other thing I'd like you to do for your legs is to push your toes down like you're squatting down in the mud or sand. 1... 2 ... 3 ... (in) 4 ... 5 ... (out). O.K. Shake the mud off. Lift up and relax. Let go your deep breath.

O.K. Now remember all those things I've told you. These little exercises, combined with your deep breathing, will help you to relax, to feel calm and peaceful.

3. Pleasant Scenes: Now to get to your pleasant scenes; yours are a campfire and sunset. What we're going to do is just practice a couple of the exercises from before. Which muscle do you want to tense today? Fist? O.K. When we get to the count of 3 while tensing the fist, take a deep breath, and at five, let it go, and then think (imagine) of your pleasant scene, sitting there watching the campfire; 1 ... 2 ... 3 ... (breathe in) 4 ... 5 ... (breathe out). As you get relaxed, sitting there watching the campfire, flames are flickering, O.K. what other muscle shall we do? Teeth? The giant jawbreaker one (count with fingers as you do exercise with child) 1 ... 2 ... 3 ... (in) 4 ... 5 ... (out). Sigh as you let your breath go. Imagine you're calmly sitting there watching the sun sink down behind the trees, the sun is setting slowly, slowly sinking down, deeper and deeper, as you get more and more relaxed.

4. Self-Sentences: The idea here is to tell yourself some sentences which will help to calm you. What can you tell yourself? (Allow child to respond). O.K. That's good. Let's go with those three. No worries (or don't worry), everything's cool (or I'm cool), and relax; I'm in control. Those are your special sentences, now I'll tell you how to do all of these things together.

5. <u>Putting it all Together</u>:   Now in order to do this all together, we're going to review each of the 12 muscles like we did in the beginning, but we're going to combine it with the breathing (taking a deep breath on 3 and letting it out on 5) and letting your muscles relax and also at the count of 5 thinking of your pleasant scene (campfire or sunset), and also telling yourself that you're calm, cool, and relaxed. O.K. now for the first one, squeeze your fists as hard as you can. 1 ... 2 ... 3 ... (breathe in) 4 ... 5 ... (breathe out). And as you let out your breath, think of your pleasant scene (peaceful sunset) and say to yourself that I'm calm and cool. Do this for each of the other muscle groups (arms, jaws, lips, nose, neck, shoulders, back, stomach, thighs, calves), but tensing each muscle as you breathe out you think of your pleasant scene and say your sentence to yourself. After you practice this a while, you will feel like a new person, and you will be able to go about doing whatever you want to do in a calm and relaxed way.

B Parent Education:
An Annotated Bibliography

Axline, V. Dibs: In search of self. Boston: Houghton Mifflin, 1964.
A moving account of the struggles of a six-year-old child to find his place in the sun. Highlights the importance of parent-child relationships.

Bach, G. R., & Wyden, P. The intimate enemy. New York: Morrow, 1969.
A useful book when parents want to learn how to fight fairly. It is really a book about controlled communication between spouses.

Bettelheim, B. Dialogue with mothers. New York: Avon, 1962.
Regardless of the title, this book is for both mothers and fathers. Written by a famous psychoanalyst, it deals with helping parents to examine their own feelings about how they wish their children to be and offers constructive discussion on how they can proceed in helping their children to develop in a manner consistent with their desires.

Braga, J., & Braga, L. Growing with children. Englewood Cliffs, N.J.: Prentice-Hall, 1974.
Growing with children is an anthology of short readings and essays by the Bragas and other experts on child development and growth. These readings emphasize what kinds of factors are important and contribute to the development of a healthy self-concept.

Braga, J., & Braga, L. Children and adults: Activities for growing together. Englewood Cliffs, N. J.: Prentice-Hall, 1976.
Written by two very eminent developmental psychologists who have in recent years contributed much to the area of child psychology, this book provides both information and activities relating to positive personal growth of both parent and child at each important phase of the child's life. Chocked full of enjoyable activities and tasks which promote the kind of positive self-assurance necessary for coping with stresses of the modern world.

126

Brutten, M., Richardson, S. O., & Manuel, G. Something's wrong with my
child. New York: Harcourt Brace Jovanovich, 1973.
A useful book for parents of a child with learning disabilities.
Utilizing the team (i.e., psychologist, physician, educator), it presents
a balanced approach to this type (L.D.) of child.

Corsini, R., & Painter, G. The practical parent: ABCs of child discipline.
New York: Harper & Row, 1975.
Described by the authors as a book "for normal parents with normal
children with normal problems," The Practical Parent is a "cookbook"
approach to solving those annoying kinds of problems that don't seem
severe enough to warrant professional concern. Throughout the book,
specific kinds of problems are identified with fundamental principles
for handling the problems via means which also encourage the child to
develop a sense of responsibility as well as alleviating the problem
behavior.

Cott, A. Fasting: The ultimate diet. New York: Bantam Books, 1975.
Dr. Cott presents discussion on the methods and benefits of controlled
fasting and its impact on both physical and mental health. Emphasiz-
ing that fasting is not starving and the importance of medical
supervision, Cott describes in detail the methods, procedures, and
considerations related to effective fasting.

Dale, R. A. Games to sing and play. New York: Scholastic, 1971.
A small booklet describing a variety of games children can play with
accompaniment of music or song. Instructions supplemented by
diagrams and pictures by Olivia H. H. Cole. Instructions are quite
simple and provide a source of expressive entertainment and
recreational activity for small children.

Dinkmeyer, D., & McKay, G. Raising a responsible child: Practical steps to
successful family relationships. New York: Simon & Schuster, 1973.
This book was written to help parents achieve a democratic family
atmosphere which enables children to develop responsible habits and
coping skills. The authors describe patterns of behavior and their
causes, and suggest a variety of attitudes and habits parents can adopt
to foster healthy family development.

Dodson, F. How to parent. New York: New American Library, 1971.
Here, Dr. Dodson shares both his experiences as a parent and opinions
as a psychologist. He describes children in terms of their developmental stages and the accompanying kinds of issues and problems that
arise at each stage. Also discussed are both general and specific
means for attending to children's problems and development. Many
common myths about child raising are dispelled and replaced with
sound advice and information. Rather comprehensive.

Dreikurs, R., Gould, S., & Corsini, R. Family Council. Chicago: Regnery,
1974.
Described as "The Dreikurs technique for putting an end to war
between parents and children (and between children and children)", the

authors present the principles and practices of a method where the family can learn to work together in sorting out and working through the problems and issues which arise in the family and between its members. The method is presented in a clear, step-by-step manner and includes examples to guide the family in developing a democratic approach to problem solving.

Dreikurs, R., & Grey, L. A parent's guide to child discipline. New York: Hawthorne, 1970.

In this book, Dreikurs and Grey discuss a practical means of solving difficulties encountered with children through the use of what are described as "natural and logical consequences". Such consequences are those which arise from or are related to the problem behavior in such a way as to help the child become more aware of his own responsibility for its occurrence, thus reducing the chance of future difficulties.

Dreikurs, R., & Soltz,V. Children: The challenge. New York: Hawthorne, 1964.

In this delightful book, the late Rudolf Dreikurs, an eminent and respected child psychiatrist, presents guidelines for parents in helping them provide a growth enhancing environment for children. Dreikurs outlines several basic principles for dealing with and understanding children's misbehavior and suggests practical ways of guiding the child to more responsible functioning.

Ellis, A., & Harper, R. A. A new guide to rational living. Hollywood, Calif.: Wilshire, 1975.

Written for adults, this book is designed to help the reader in understanding how his/her own irrational thinking and believing leads to unhappiness and tension. The authors describe a method by which people can, through their own conscious effort, understand and remedy their own irrational thinking, creating a more stable and harmonious way of living and coping.

Feingold, B. F. Why your child is hyperactive. New York: Random House, 1975.

Dr. Feingold, a pediatrician and allergist, reveals the role of food additives and diet in contributing to children's hyperactivity. He discusses both cases and research which reveal that many of the foods we ingest very frequently produce remarkable and often negative personality changes in children. In addition, Dr. Feingold offers specific advice on a diet which has had rather dramatic success in alleviating hyperactive symptoms.

Fredericks, C. Carlton Fredericks' high-fiber way to total health. New York: Pocket Books, 1976.

The author not only discusses the health benefits of a diet high in fiber, but also addresses the issue of diet and nutrition in general. Not a cultist or fanatical viewpoint, rather, some seemingly sound and well documented information on foods and their contribution (and detriment) to health.

Gesell, A., & Ilg, F. L. The child from five to ten. New York: Harper & Row, 1946.
   This book, for parents and professionals, describes the growth patterns and behaviors characteristic of the child as he/she moves through the years from five to ten.   The authors treat each year as having distinctive characteristics and describes these characteristics in great detail.

Gesell, A., Ilg, F. L., & Ames, L.B. The years from ten to sixteen. New York: Harper & Row, 1956.
   This book, written by three prominent experts in the field of human development, has value for both parents and professionals.   It is devoted to detailed descriptions of the important aspects of growth during the preadolescent and adolescent years. Although not problem oriented, the book may help the reader to better understand the characteristics and behavior patterns of the youth as she or he moves through the adolescent years.

Ginott, H. Between parent and child. New York: Avon, 1965.
   In easily understandable terms, Dr. Haim Ginott describes ways of encouraging the child's positive growth and reducing his/her anxiety and self-defeating patterns of behavior through particular ways of talking, listening, and responding.   Through such communication the parent can help the child to feel more understood as well as accepted and encouraged.

Gordon, T. P.E.T.: Parent effectiveness training. New York: Wyden, 1970.
   In P.E.T., Thomas Gordon describes what he calls the "no lose" method of parenting, a method designed to help parents break through communication barriers between themselves and their children. Gordon candidly identifies common roadblocks to communication and offers parents specific kinds of techniques for effectively talking with and listening to their children.

Gutwirth, S. W. You can learn to relax. Hollywood, Calif.: Wilshire, 1968.
   Dr. Gutwirth explains how persons can, through systematic practice, attain complete relaxation and greater freedom from tension and anxiety.   A step-by-step method that teaches the reader to focus on one muscle area at a time, gradually working through all the muscles in the body.

Hauck, P. A. The rational management of children. New York: Libra, 1972.
   A book which combines both the rational and Dreikurian approaches to child raising. It is useful for parents who are cognitively oriented and deals with a variety of fears, anger, worry, undesirable habits, and discipline.

Hauck, P. Overcoming depression. Philadelphia: The Westminster Press, 1973.
   A very readable book on how people are essentially trained to be neurotic and depressed and how they can retrain themselves to be better adjusted persons. Hauck identifies three principal reasons why

people get depressed and describes ways to go about overcoming these three conditions through learning new ways of thinking.

Keat, D. B. Fundamentals of child counseling. Boston: Houghton Mifflin, 1974.

A textbook on counseling children in the school. Provides comprehensive information on both the many functions of the elementary school counselor and techniques and methods for promoting positive child development. One of the most complete treatments to date on the subject of child counseling.

Keat, D. B., & Guerney, L. What every parent needs to know about raising children. University Park, Pa.: Cope Press, 1978.

This book combines the most useful parenting procedures from other writers with the authors' own unique approaches. The result is a presentation of 50 parenting procedures from which you will find something to suit any situation with which you are confronted.

Larrick, N. A parent's guide to children's reading. New York: Bantam, 1975.

Written by a well-known authority on children's reading and education, this book is designed to provide practical suggestions and information on enhancement of children's reading. Much discussion is devoted to the kinds of elements that influence and contribute to children's reading ability, guidelines for selecting material for enhancing children's reading ability, and identification of specific books which appeal to children's varied interests.

Lazarus, A. A. Daily living: Coping with tensions and anxieties: Relaxation exercises I, II, and III. Chicago: Instructional Dynamics, 1970.

A series of cassettes designed to aid the listener in attaining complete body relaxation. Moving from the relaxation of specific muscles to more complex and total kinds of relaxation, Lazarus provides the kind of taped atmosphere which contributes to the learning of methods proved effective in providing freedom from damaging tension.

Lazarus, A. A. Learning to relax. New York: Institute for Rational Living, 1975.

Famous psychologist and psychotherapist Arnold Lazarus describes how to alleviate tension and anxiety through muscle relaxation techniques. A step-by-step procedure of immense value in remedying the detrimental effects of stress.

Lazarus, A., & Fay, A. I can if I want to. New York: Morrow, 1975.

This short, well-written book points out how, through certain common mistakes people make in their thinking, people make themselves unhappy. The authors describe these mistaken and faulty assumptions and offer step-by-step means for developing habits in thinking and behavior for a more healthy and assertive way of life.

LeCron, L. The complete guide to hypnosis. New York: Barnes & Noble, 1971.

An easy reading book on the subject of hypnosis. The author describes the essential nature of hypnosis and its useful application. In doing so, he attempts to dispell many of the myths and magical notions that often surround the subject and provides answers to many questions commonly asked about it. A seemingly good introduction to hypnosis.

Moustakas, C. Who will listen? New York: Ballantine, 1975.
Clark Moustakas, renowned child psychologist and psychotherapist, writes on the nature of communication between parents and children and the impact of genuine understanding on the process of growth in both parent and child. Moustakas essentially identifies the elements crucial to an understanding parent-child relationship and describes several cases that illustrate both how the process of communication and self-expression contributes to growth.

Patterson, G. R. Families. Champaign, Ill.: Research Press, 1971.
A small, handy, programmed book which provides parents with social learning approaches to family life. Some of the specific procedures covered are contracting and time out. Special applications to the problem areas of aggression and noncompliance are presented.

Patterson, G. R., & Gullion, M. E. Living with children: New methods for parents and teachers. Champaign, Ill.: Research Press, 1968.
This is the parent's primer (we usually use it before Families because it is somewhat simpler) in the evolution of Patterson's approaches. Of special interest are the programmed chapters on the following children: fighter, negativistic, hyperactive, dependent, frightened, and withdrawn.

Robertiello, R. Hold them very close, then let them go. New York: The Dial Press, 1975.
Dr. Robertiello relies on recent research in child development to offer advice to parents on how to raise children to be both loving and productive. Discussion revolves around how parents can help the child grow into a responsible, productive and authentic adult by a gradual allowance of independence and autonomy rather than unrestricted or unquestioned permissiveness.

Simon, S. B., & Olds, S. W. Helping your child learn right from wrong: A guide to values clarification. New York: Simon & Schuster, 1976.
This is perhaps the first book on the market exclusively devoted to helping families work together in systematically identifying their needs, feelings, and desires. The book first discusses the importance of clarifying values in terms of problem-solving and decision making and then describes in detail specific exercises and strategies designed to help members of familes to know themselves and each other better.

Stuart, R. B., & Davis, B. Slim chance in a fat world. Champaign, Ill.: Research Press, 1972.
This book describes a method of weight reduction that has shown great promise in "girth control." Using the technique of behavior modification outlined in this text, the chances of safe weight loss are quite probable. A comprehensive coverage of specific methods and things to consider in controlling obesity. Much supporting research is cited.

Van Lysebeth, A. Yoga self-taught. New York: Barnes & Noble, 1973.
    A seemingly comprehensive manual for the correct and safe practice
    of yoga. Both the benefits and methods of yoga are described and
    supplemented by drawings, photographs, and diagrams. Presented as
    an effective means of attaining deep relaxation and relief from
    tension, the book is written for the beginner who hasn't had the
    opportunity for formal instruction.

Wittenberg, H. Isometrics. New York: Award, 1964.
    This paperback provides photographic illustrations and instruction in a
    form of physical exercise designed to build and strengthen muscles.
    The book outlines different plans for different age and fitness levels.

Yudkin, T. Sweet and dangerous. New York: Bantam, 1972.
    This is a book which describes the relationship between sugar intake
    and poor health. Yudkin, a very distinguished and renowned scientist,
    emphatically reveals why the ordinary table sugar that millions of
    Americans ingest today is a crucial health hazard. Written in clear
    and concise terms with much food for thought.

C Child Bibliotherapy and Audiotherapy

Bedford, S. Instant replay. New York: Institute for Rational Living, 1974.
Presented as "a method of counseling and communicating with people." Instant replay is a short book, accompanied by an instruction manual, which describes a step-by-step way of going back over past events and "rough spots", and sorting out the feelings, behaviors, and consequences that occurred. The method is designed to help the person further understand what went on and how constructive changes can be made to reduce anxiety and avoid future rough spots.

deSchweinitz, K. Growing up. New York: Macmillan, 1965.
This book tells how animals and people are born and grow up. It is offered to parents and other adults as help in answering conversationally the questions which younger children ask about reproduction, birth, and growth of human beings.

Dorough, R. Multiplication rock. Los Angeles: American Broadcasting Company, 1973.
A songbook containing words and music from the ABC television series, Multiplication Rock. Contains delightful melodies and words designed not just to keep kids' feet tapping, but to teach (from age three on up) them mathematical concepts as well. There is also a Capitol (SJA-11174) record available which presents all of the songs.

Freed, A. TA for kids (and other grownups too). Sacramento, Calif.: Jalmar Press, 1971.
A book primarily for boys and girls in grades 3-6, TA for kids explains and illustrates, in short words and simple phrases, the basic concepts of Transactional Analysis, a method for better understanding how and why people behave and feel the way they do. This book is an aid to helping children to identify and express their inner feelings.

Freed, A. TA for tots (and other prinzes). Sacramento, Calif.: Jalmar Press, 1973.

This is a delightful book written to help small children identify and express their feelings about things. It is presented in storybook form with pleasing cartoons and simple text which can be easily read to or by children.

Gardner, R. The boys and girls book about divorce. New York: Bantam, 1970.

In clear and straightforward language, Dr. Gardner has written for youngsters in order to help them better understand the kinds of difficult feelings, thoughts and behaviors that usually accompany marital dissolution. Practical advice is given on how to handle one's self through what is a terribly difficult time for parents and youngsters alike. In offering such comments, Dr. Gardner helps both parents and children to better accept many of the things that go on inside themselves as natural responses to a complex and disruptive situation.

Gardner, R. Dr. Gardner's stories about the real world. Englewood Cliffs, N.J.: Prentice-Hall, 1972.

Here again, the writings of Dr. Gardner provide a therapeutic, growth-enhancing vehicle for children. This is a book of stories about the kinds of conflicts and problems not uncommonly encountered by children. Written with a flavor quite appealing to children, the book provides a variety of conflict situations oriented toward happenings in the real world rather than toward strict fantasy, which is often the case with fables designed to convey an important message.

Gardner, R. MBD: The family book about minimal brain dysfunction. New York: Aronson, 1973.

This book is addressed to both youngsters and their parents and in a clear, straightforward manner, discusses what minimal brain dysfunction (learning disabilities, hyperactivity) is and how to deal with difficulties it presents. Many common misconceptions of minimal brain dysfunction are dispelled.

Gardner, R. Dr. Gardner's fairy tales for today's children. Englewood Cliffs, N. J.: Prentice-Hall, 1974.

Dr. Gardner has assembled a collection of stories designed to capture the imagination of children and provide them with meaningful "food for thought". Unlike most common fairy tales or myths, these stories relate to the real world and characteristic problems of the people in it. The text is supplemented by appealing illustrations.

Grollman, E. A. Talking about death. Boston: Beacon Press, 1970.

This small paperback book is a dialogue between a parent and child about death. It represents an effort to guide a child toward the meaning of this inevitable happening which we all must deal with. Although the example used is the death of grandfather, the meaning of death as well as the importance of talking to someone who will listen to you is generalizable to other losses.

Hart, C., Pogrebin, L. C., Rogers, M., & Thomas, M. Free to be, you and me. New York: McGraw-Hill, 1974.

A delightful album of songs designed to dispell many of the myths created by a sexually biased culture. It can be appreciated by both kids and adults and features songs by many celebrities of TV and film. Available in both songbook and record forms.

Kalb, J., & Viscott, D. What every kid should know. Boston: Houghton-Mifflin, 1976.

Written in an appealing and easily understood style, this book explains why youngsters often feel inadequate and offers ways in which kids can better know themselves and deal more effectively with feelings which contribute to negative self-images. The book deals with a wide variety of areas of concern to kids today, including issues surrounding divorce, and can be read and enjoyed by both adults and youngsters.

LeShan, E. What makes me feel this way? Growing up with human emotions. New York: Collier, 1972.

A book for young persons specifically written to help them understand about the range of feelings that humans experience. Written in very appealing and understandable terms, the book discusses the influence of feelings on personal adjustment and how they affect our everyday behavior. Generally, the theme of the book revolves around the premise that we have all kinds of feelings, and that these are natural and should not produce fear or shame.

Palmer, H. Getting to know myself. Freeport, N. Y.: Educational Activities, 1972.

An enjoyable record which uses movement-oriented activities (set to music) to help a child to become aware of his/her body, its parts, the physical environment, his/her feelings and emotions. The feelings songs focus on the emotions of being happy, sad, angry, and afraid. Another song deals with getting to know peers and the encouragement of children to be friends.

Pomeroy, W. Boys and sex. New York: Delacorte Press, 1968.

Written primarily for boys entering adolescence, this book addresses the difficulties often encountered with sexual development. Dr. Pomeroy discusses in frank yet sensitive terms the factors involved in boys' sexual behavior and provides information designed to alleviate the fear, anxiety, and shame young males sometimes associate with their entrance to puberty.

Pomeroy, W. Girls and sex. New York: Dell, 1969.

This book is the sequel to Pomeroy's Boys and Sex. It provides information relating to girls' sexual development in a sensitive and informative manner. Designed to alleviate fears often attendent to the onset of female puberty, it is both objective and enlightening.

Rogers, F. Mister Rogers' songbooks. New York: Random House, 1970.
    A book filled with words and music written by Mr. Rogers of children's
    television fame. These songs relate to the many kinds of feelings that
    both children and adults share and provides a creative means for
    fostering self-expression for both parent and child. The songs reflect
    much tenderness and warmth. Fred Rogers has also produced
    numerous records for children (e.g., Misterogers Knows That You Are
    Special, Small World Records, 4RS-1252).

Simon, S. I am loveable and capable. Niles, Illinois. Argus Communications,
    1973.
    A short book written for both youngsters and adults which demon-
    strates how one's self-esteem can be torn down through the course of
    daily living. It points up that the way one sees oneself is an important
    element in how he or she functions in life. The book also reveals how
    people whose esteem has suffered can be easily put down and how such
    put-downs are destructive forces to the human spirit.

Widerberg, S. The kids own XYZ of love and sex. New York: Stein & Day,
    1973.
    Specifically written for children from seven to 13, this book provides
    sexual information relating to questions very commonly asked by
    children. It is simply and well written and tastefully illustrated. Can
    be of great assistance to parents in explaining sex to their children.

D Adolescent Bibliotherapy

Freed, A.M., T. A. for teens. Sacramento, Calif.: Jalmar Press, 1976.

Gardner, R.A., The boys and girls book about divorce. New York: Science House, 1971.

Gnagey, T.D., How to put up with parents: A guide for teenagers. Champaign, Ill.: Research Press, 1975.

Gordon, S., & Conant, R., You. New York: Quadrangle, 1975.

Gutwirth, S.W., , You can learn to relax. Hollywood, Calif.: Wilshire, 1968.

James, M., & Jongeward, D., Born to win. Reading, Mass.: Addison-Wesley, 1971.

King, M., For we are. Reading, Mass.: Addison-Wesley, 1975.

Lazarus, A., & Fay, A., I can if I want to. New York: Morrow, 1975.

Mayle, P., Robins, A., & Walter, P., What's happening to me? Secaucus, N.J.: Stuart, 1975.

Minick, M., The kung fu exercise book. New York: Simon Schuster, 1964.

Pomeroy, W., Boys and sex. New York: Delacorte, 1960.

Pomeroy, W., Girls and sex. New York: Dell, 1969.

Prather, H., Notes to myself. New York: Bantam Books, 1976.

Richards, A., & Willis, I., How to get it together when your parents are coming apart. New York: David McKay, 1976.

Simon, S., I am loveable and capable. Niles, Ill.: Argus Communications, 1973.

Wrenn, C. G., & Schwarzrock, S., Parents can be a problem. Circle Pines, Minn.: American Guidance Service, 1970.

Young, H. S., A rational counseling primer. New York: Institute for Rational Living, 1974.

E

Basic Id Classroom Materials: DUSO

This abridged appendix reflects how stories in DUSO I (Dinkmeyer, 1970) can be coded for their primary and secondary modes. In addition, to aid one in selecting relevant stories, a brief summary is provided. For the complete multimodal coding system on DUSO and FOCUS I, II, III, the interested reader is invited to contact one of the above authors (Barbara Green, Penn State University, 313 Carpenter Building, University Park, Pennsylvania 16802).

Unit I - Intro (B, IR)

The Underwater Problem Solvers

About the methods DUSO and his friends use to solve problems. Rules include Raise Your Hand; Listen Carefully; Don't Clam Up; Stick to the Point; and Think Together.

Unit I - A (I, C)

The Red and White Bluebird

DUSO meets a red and white checkered bird who insists she is blue. The point is made that you are the only one in the world like you.

Unit I - B (IR, B)

The Fairfield Fire Department

The four firemen of a small town each have different occupations, but can work together as a team on the fire department.

Unit I - C (A, B)

Dizzy Terry

Terry uses his dizzy spells to get attention. DUSO helps him see that there are other appropriate ways to gain attention.

Unit I - D (A, I)

Frowny Browny

Frowny is a boy with a dejected appearance who is sure nobody likes him. He finds a little girl who is lost, and in trying to cheer her up discovers he can forget himself and have fun.

Unit I - E (IR, B)

The Box

Two girls can't play with the group of children they want to. Both find old crates on the way home, one sits in it and cries while the other finds a way to play in it.

Unit II - Intro (IR, A)

DUSO Talks About Friends

DUSO shares stories about his underwater friends to illustrate everyone needs to have friends; friends help each other; the best way to make friends is to try to understand how others feel.

Unit II - A (IR, B)

Gordo and Molly

Brian helps settle a dispute between Gordo and Molly by helping them learn to share.

Unit II - B (A, IR)

You Don't Love Me Anymore

Mary Ann is punished and sent to her room. She thinks she was punished because her mom doesn't love her, but her mom recalls a time they punished her dog and Mary Ann understands.

Unit II - C (IR, B)

Peeper

Peeper, a baby chick, is put in a new cage, tries to be friendly only to get pecked. A new chick is put in the cage and Peeper won't peck her like the rest.

Unit II - D (IR,B)

The Outsider

Best friends fight over the acceptance of a new friend.

F Helping Classroom Exercise

Materials:

    For each student, a pack of seven (7) cards (3 x 5), mixed together and blank side up. The cards each have one letter of the sentence, "I'm great!" written on one side.

Directions to Students:

1. Look only at the blank side until directed to turn the cards over.

2. As each of the following directions is given, you will write the answers, one to a card, on the blank side of each card. You may tell the class your answers if you want. You will keep the cards at the end of the class. (Students who are not able to write the answers could take turns answering aloud and be allowed to take out one card from the pack each time they do so.)

    (H) Name something good that you do for your body.

    (E) Name something that is fun for you.

    (L) Name something good that you are learning how to do.

    (P) Write the name of somebody who treats you well.

    (I) Name something that you do well.

    (N) Name the most important thing you will do today.

    (G) Name something nice you have done for someone else.

3. Turn all your cards over and unscramble the anagram. Is it true?

<u>Objective:</u>

Given seven (7) cards each, questions and class discussion, the learners will write seven (7) positive statements about themselves and imply that they are "great" people.

1. Use this exercise to improve self-concept <u>before</u> discussing self-improvement.

2. Explain <u>HELPING,</u> refer back to this exercise. Label each card according to mode.

3. Use each letter as the theme for a separate lesson. Students could contract to work on one aspect of each mode - perhaps one mode per week until all modes have been added to the contract. They can keep a journal and/or charts of progress in each mode.

4. Have students keep the cards and read them when they need a boost to the self-image.

5. As a follow up, students can add to the stack of good things by making five more cards in various modes.

6 The cards could be duplicated onto construction paper, with I'M GREAT on one side and the incomplete sentences (e.g., _____ is a person who treats me well, etc.) on the other side (for students with minimal writing ability).

G Anxiety Management Training

A. References

Keat, D.B., Fundamentals of child counseling. Boston: Houghton Mifflin, 1974, pp. 67-68.

Krumboltz, J. F., & Thoresen, C.E. (Eds.), Behavioral counseling: Cases and techniques. New York: Holt, Rinehart & Winston, 1969, pp. 269-272.

Lazarus, A.A., Behavior therapy and beyond. New York: Wiley, 1971, pp. 273-275.

Lazarus, A. A. (Ed.) Multimodal behavior therapy. New York: Springer, 1976, pp. 103-115.

B. Bibliotherapy

Fensterheim, H., & Baer, J., Don't say yes when you want to say no. New York: Dell, 1975.

Gutwirth, S.W., You can learn to relax. Hollywood, Calif.: Wilshire, 1968.

Jacobson, E., You must relax. New York: McGraw-Hill, 1962.

Walker, C. E., Learn to relax. Englewood Cliffs, N. J.: Prentice Hall, 1975.

Assorted Tapes: Lazarus, 1970, 1975; Keat, 1977 (see references).

C. Steps. Richardson, F. C. In Lazarus, A. A. (Ed.), Multimodal behavior therapy. New York: Springer, 1976, pp. 103-115.

1. Sources of anxiety and fear are determined.
2. Fear and social anxiety inventory.
3. Diary about stressful situations.
4. Training in muscle relaxation.
5. Rational thinking training.
6. Write down alternative, calming beliefs.
7. Self-induce anxiety, competency scenes.
8. Imaginal rehearsal of unanxious coping.
9. Homework assignments to try out new strategies and behaviors.

H Imagery Treatment

A. <u>References</u> (see Chapter 11 for complete reference citations)

Ellis & Harper, 1975, pp. 210-215
Goldfried & Davison, 1976, pp. 146-147
Keat, 1974, pp. 77-78, 296-297
Krumboltz & Thoresen, 1969, pp. 319-327
Lazarus, 1971, pp. 66-81, 208-209, 226-231
Lazarus, 1972, pp. 87-99
Lazarus, 1976, pp. 37-39, 45, 90-91, 100-113, 120-121, 127, 175

B. <u>Bibliotherapy</u>

Gordon, S., & Conant, R., <u>You</u>. New York: Quadrangle, 1975.
James, M., & Jongeward, D., <u>Born to win</u>. Reading, Mass: Addison-Wesley, 1971.
Simon, S., <u>I am loveable and capable</u>. Niles, Ill.: Argus, 1973.

C. <u>Techniques</u> (see Table 11-1, Chapter 11, Imagery Section)

Emotive imagery
Thought stopping
Aversive imagery
Eidetic imagery
Time projection
Covert sensitization
One-downmanship
Empty chair
Desert island
Negative imagery
Positive imagery
Rational imagery
Implosive therapy
"As if procedure"
"Blow up technique"

Cognitive
Treatment

A. References

Beck, A.T., Cognitive therapy and the emotional disorders. New York: International Universities Press, 1976, pp. 213-337.

Goldfried, M. R., & Davison, G.C., Clinical behavior therapy. New York: Holt, Rinehart & Winston, 1976, pp. 158-185.

Keat, D.B., Fundamentals of child counseling. Boston: Houghton Mifflin, 1974, pp. 75-77.

Lazarus, A.A., Behavior therapy and beyond. New York: Wiley, 1971, pp. 180-184.

Lazarus, A.A., (Ed.) Multimodal behavior therapy. New York: Springer, 1976, pp. 39-46.

B. Bibliotherapy

Ellis, A., & Harper, R., A new guide to rational living. Englewood Cliffs, N. J.: Prentice-Hall, 1975.

Lazarus, A.A., & Fay, A., I can if I want to. New York: Morrow, 1975.

C. Steps in therapy

1. Explain basic assumptions.
2. Have client read bibliotherapy.
3. Client picks source of irrational or mistaken idea(s) for homework.
4. Help client with corrective self-talk.
5. Enact dialogues during session.
6. Use tapes and playbacks to improve rational self-corrections.
7. Deal with developing a more rational philosophy of living.

J Interpersonal Treatment

A. <u>References</u>

Keat, D.B., <u>Fundamentals of child counseling</u>. Boston: Houghton Mifflin, 1974, pp. 88, 138, 147-159, 163, 255-256.

Lazarus, A.A., <u>Behavior therapy and beyond</u>. New York: Wiley, 1971, pp. 137-139, 212-214.

Lazarus, A. A. (Ed.), <u>Multimodal behavior therapy</u>. New York: Springer, 1976, pp. 41-43, 100-101, 121-122, 128-129, 176-177.

B. <u>Bibliotherapy</u>

Bach, G., & Goldberg, H. <u>Creative aggression</u>. New York: Doubleday, 1974.

Bedford, S., <u>Instant replay</u>. New York: Institute for Rational Living, 1974.

Dreikurs, R., Gould S., & Corsini, R.J., <u>Family council</u>. Chicago: Regnery, 1974.

Gordon, T., <u>Parent effectiveness training</u>. New York: Wyden, 1970.

Knox, D., <u>Marriage happiness</u>. Champaign, Ill.: Research Press, 1971.

Wahlroos, S., <u>Family communication</u>. New York: Signet, 1974.

C. <u>Techniques</u> (see Chapter 11, Table 1, Interpersonal Section)

Communications training
Friendship training
Transactional analysis
Buddy programs
Family council meetings

References

Ackerman, J.M., Operant conditioning techniques for the classroom teacher. Glennview, Ill.: Scott, Foresman, 1972.

Adams, R., & Murray, R., Megavitamin therapy. New York: Larchmont, 1973.

Ahsen, A., Eidetic parents test and analysis. New York: Brandon House, 1972.

Ahsen, A., & Lazarus, A.A., Eidetics: An internal behavior approach. In Lazarus, A.A. (Ed.), Clinical behavior therapy. New York: Brunner/Mazel, 1972. Pp. 87-95.

Akins, W.R., & Nurnberg, H.G., How to meditate without attending a TM class. New York: Crown, 1976.

Alberti, R.E., & Emmons, M.L., Your perfect right. San Luis Obispo, Calif.: IMPACT, 1974.

American Association of School Administrators, Washington, D.C., Imperatives in Education. Report of the AASA Commission on Imperatives in Education, 1966.

Andronico, M.P., & Guerney, B., The potential application of filial therapy to the school situation. Journal of School Psychology, 1967, 6, 2-7.

Authier, J., Gustafson, K., Guerney, B., & Kasdorf, J., The psychological practitioner as a teacher: A theoretical, historical and practical review. The Counseling Psychologist, 1975, 1, 31-52.

Azrin, N.H., & Nunn, R.G., Habit reversal: A method of eliminating nervous habits and tics. Behaviour Research and Therapy, 1973. 11, 619-628.

Bach, G.R., & Goldberg, H., Creative aggression: The art of assertive living. New York: Doubleday, 1974.

Bandura, A., Principles of behavior modification. New York: Holt, 1969.

Barclay, J.R., The Barclay classroom climate inventory. Lexington, Ky.: Educational Skills Development, 1972.

Baruth, L.G., & Phillips, M.W., Bibliotherapy and the school counselor. The School Counselor, 1976, 23, 191-199.

Bedford, S., Instant replay. New York: Institute for Rational Living, 1974.

Bellak, L., Bellak, S.S., & Hurvich, M.S., Children's appreception test -Human figures. Larchmont, N.Y.,: C.P.S., 1965.

Bender, L., A visual motor Gestalt test and its clinical use. New York: American Orthopsychiatric Association, 1938.

Bender, L., Bender motor Gestalt test. Cards and manual of instructions. New York: American Orthopsychiatric Association, 1946.

Bennett, G.K., Seashore, H.G., & Wesman, A.G., Differential attitude tests. New York: The Psychological Corporation, 1972.

Bennett, M.E., Guidance in groups. New York: McGraw-Hill, 1963.

Benton, A. The revised visual retention test. New York: The Psychological Corporation, 1963.

Berne, E. Games people play. New York: Grove Press, 1964.

Bessell, H., & Palomares, U., Methods in human development. LaMesa, Calif.: Human Development Training Institute, 1973.

Biehn, J., Community as counselor. Personnel and Guidance Journal, 1972, 50, 730-734.

Blackham, G., & Silberman, A., Modification of child behavior. Belmont, Calif.: Wadsworth, 1971.

Blackham, G., & Silberman, A., Modification of child and adolescent behavior (2nd edition). Belmont, Calif.: Wadsworth, 1975.

Bloomfield, H., Cain, P.C., Jaffe, D.T., & Kory, R.B., TM: Discovering inner energy and overcoming stress. New York: Dell, 1975.

Bonny, H.L., & Savary, L.M., Music and your mind. New York: Harper & Row, 1973.

Bonsall, M.R., Meyers, C.E., & Thorpe, L.P., What I like to do. Chicago: Science Research Associates, 1958.

Boria, M.C., The miracle of sex. Sydney, Australia: Patrician, 1970.

Bower, S., Amatea, E., & Anderson, R., Assertiveness training with children. Elementary School Guidance and Counseling, 1976, 10, 236-245.

Brammer, L.M., & Shostrom, E.L., Therapeutic psychology. Englewood Cliffs, N.J.,: Prentice-Hall, 1968.

Bratcher, R.G., Good news for the modern man: The new testament in today's English version. (3rd Ed.) Hawthorne, N.J.: American Bible Society, 1971.

Brown, G.I., Human teaching for human learning: An introduction to confluent education. New York: Viking Press, 1971.

Brown, W.F., Student-to-student counseling for academic adjustment. Personnel and Guidance Journal, 1965, 43, 811-816.

Bry, A., The TA primer. New York: Perennial Library, 1973.

Bry, A., TA games. New York: Perennial Library, 1975.

Bry, A., TA for families. New York: Perennial Library, 1976.

Canfield, J., & Wells, H.C., 100 ways to enhance self-concept in the classroom. Englewood Cliffs, N.J.: Prentice-Hall, 1976.

Carkhuff, R.R., Differential functioning of lay and professional helpers. Journal of Counseling Psychology, 1968, 15, 117-126.

Carkhuff, R.R., Helping and human relations: A primer for lay and professional helpers. Volume I Selection and Training. New York: Holt, Rinehart & Winston, 1969a.

Carkhuff, R.R., Helping and human relations: A primer for lay and professional helpers. Volume 2 Practice and Research. New York: Holt, Rinehart & Winston, 1969b.

Carkhuff, R.R., & Bierman, R., Training as a preferred mode of treatment for parents of emotionally disturbed children. Journal of Counseling Psychology, 1970, 17, 157-161.

Carkhuff, R.R., The art of problem solving. Amherst, Mass.: Human Development Press, 1973.

Cautela, J.R., & Kastenbaum, R., A reinforcement survey schedule for use in therapy, training and research. Psychological Reports, 1967, 20, 1115-1130.

Chase, S., & Whitbread, J., How to help your child get the most out of school. New York: Dell, 1974.

Clay, V.S., Children deal with death. School Counselor, 1976, 23, 175-184.

Comfort, A., The joy of sex. New York: Crown, 1972.

Cooper, K.H., Aerobics. New York: Bantam, 1968.

Cooper, K.H., The new aerobics. New York: Bantam, 1970.

Cooper, M., & Cooper, K.H., Aerobics for women. New York: Bantam, 1972.

Coopersmith, S., The antecedents of self-esteem. San Francisco: W.H. Freeman, 1967.

Cornish, R.D., & Dilley, J.S., Comparison of three methods to reduce test anxiety. Journal of Counseling Psychology, 1973, 20 (6), 499-503.

Coorigan, R., A peer help center. Personnel and Guidance Journal, 1974. 53, 329-330.

Corsini, R.J., & Painter, G., The practical parent. New York: Harper & Row, 1975.

Cott, A., Treatment of learning disabilities. Journal of Orthomolecular Psychiatry, 1974, 3, 343,355.

Cott, A., Fasting: The ultimate diet. New York: Bantam Books, 1975.

Danish, S., & Hauer, A.L., Helping skills: A basic training program. New York: Human Sciences Press, 1973.

Danskin, D.G., & Walters, E.D., Biofeedback and voluntary self-regulation: Counseling and education. Personnel and Guidance Journal, 1973, 51, 633-638.

Dinkmeyer, D., Developing understanding of self and others (DUSO, D-1). Circle Pines, Minn.: American Guidance Service, 1970.

Dinkmeyer, D., & McKay, B., Raising a responsible child. New York: Simon & Schuster, 1973.

Doll, E.A., The measurement of social competence. Minneapolis, Minn.: Educational Test Bureau, 1953.

Doll, E.A., Preschool attainment record. Circle Pines, Minn.: American Guidance Service, 1966.

Downing, C.J., Teaching children behavior change techniques. Elementary School Guidance and Counseling, 1977, 11, 277-283.

Dreikurs, R., Psychology in the classroom. New York: Harper, 1968.

Dreikurs, R., Gould, S., & Corsini, R., Family council. Chicago: Henry Regnery, 1974.

Dreikurs, R., & Soltz, V., Children: The challenge. New York: Hawthorne, 1964.

Dunn, L.M., Peabody picture vocabulary test. Circle Pines, Minn.: American Guidance Service, 1965.

Dyer, W.W., Your erroneous zones. New York: Funk & Wagnalls, 1976.

Ellis, A., Reason and emotion in psychotherapy. New York: Stuart, 1962.

Ellis, A., The intelligent woman's guide to man-hunting. New York: Stuart, 1965.

Ellis, A., Comments on C.H. Patterson's "current view of client-centered or relationship therapy." The Counseling Psychologist, 1969, 1, 37-42.

Ellis, A., How to stubbornly refuse to be ashamed of anything (tape). New York: Institute for Rational Living, 1972.

Ellis, A., Humanistic psychology: The rational-emotive approach. New York: Julian Press, 1973.

Ellis, A., & Harper, R.A., A new guide to rational living. Englewood Cliffs, N.J.: Prentice-Hall, 1975.

Evans, F.L., & Gilmartin, A.L., Art encounter--A child's eye view. Elementary School Journal, 1976, 76, 272-275.

Fasting, B.P., Children's world friendship. Elementary School Journal, 1975, 76, 100-103.

Feingold, B.F., Why your child is hyperactive. New York: Random House, 1975.

Fernsterheim, H., & Baer, J., Don't say yes when you want to say no. New York: Dell, 1975.

Ferreira, L., Dance: An adjunct to group counseling. In M. Ohlsen (Ed.), Counseling children in groups. New York: Holt, Rinehart, & Winston, 1973. Pp. 95-115.

Fo, W.S.O., & O'Donnell, C.R., The buddy system: Relationship and contingency conditions in a community intervention program for youth with nonprofessionals as behavior change agents. Journal of Consulting and Clinical Psychology, 1974, 42, 163-169.

Forer, B.R., The Forer structured sentence completion test. Santa Monica, Calif.: Western Psychological Services, 1957.

Frank, M., Ferdinand, B., & Bailey, W., Peer group counseling: A challenge to grow. The School Counselor, 1975, 22, 267-272.

Fredericks, C., Nutrition: Your key to good health. North Hollywood, Calif.: London Press, 1964.

Fredericks, C., Carlton Fredericks' high-fiber way to total health. New York: Pocket Books, 1976.

Freed, A.M., T.A. for tots. Sacramento, Calif.: Jalmar Press, 1973.

Freed, A.M., T.A. for teens. Sacramento, Calif.: Jalmar Press, 1976.

Frostig, M., Lefever, W., & Wittlesey, J., Developmental test of visual perception. Palo Alto, Calif.: Consulting Psychologists Press, 1966.

Frostig, M., The developmental program in visual perception. Chicago: Follett, 1966.

Furman, E. (Ed.), A child's parent dies. New Haven: Yale University Press, 1974.

Gade, E.M., & Goodman, R.E., Vocational preferences of daughters of alcoholics. Vocational Guidance Quarterly, 1975, 24, 41-47.

Garcia, E.J., & Pellegrini, N., Homer the homely hound. New York: Institute for Rational Living, 1974.

Gardner, R.A., The boys and girls book about divorce. New York: Institute for Rational Living, 1970.

Gardner, R.A., Dr. Gardner's stories about the real world. Englewood Cliffs, N.J.: Prentice-Hall, 1972.

Gardner, R.A., The talking, feeling and doing game. Cresskill, N.J.: Creative Therapeutics, 1973.

Gardner, R.A., Dr. Gardner's fairy tales for today's children. Englewood Cliffs, N.J.: Prentice-Hall, 1974.

Gardner, R.A., Dr. Gardner talks to boys and girls about divorce. New York: Psychotherapy Tape Library, 1975.

Gardner, R.A., Dr. Gardner talks to divorced parents. (tape). New York: Psychotherapy Tape Library, 1975.

Gardner, R.A., Psychotherapeutic approaches to the resistant child. New York: Jason Aronson, 1975.

Gerler, E.R., The Magic Circle program: How to involve teachers. Elementary School Guidance and Counseling, 1973, 8, 86-91.

Gerler, E.R., The "BASIC ID" in career education. Vocational Guidance Quarterly, 1977, 25, 238-244.

Gerler, E.R., & Keat, D.B., Multimodal education: Treating the "BASIC ID" of the elementary school classroom. The Humanist Educator, 1977, 15, 148-154.

Gerler, E.R., & Pepperman, C.W., Children's reactions to small group psychological education. Together: Journal of the Association for Specialists in Group Work, 1976, 1, 40-47.

Giles, J.R., Positive peer culture in the public school system. The National Association of Secondary School Principals, 1975, 59, 22-28.

Ginott, H., Group psychotherapy with children. New York: McGraw-Hill, 1961.

Glasser, W., Schools without failure. New York: Harper & Row, 1969.

Glasser, W., Positive addiction. New York: Harper & Row, 1976.

Goldfried, M.R., & Davison, G.C., Clinical behavior therapy. New York: Holt, Rinehart & Winston, 1976.

Goodman, G., Companionship therapy. San Francisco: Jossey Bass, 1972.

Gordon, S., & Conant, R., You. New York: Quadrangle, 1975.

Gordan, T., Teacher effectiveness training. New York: Wyden, 1974.

Graham, R., Moral education: A child's right to a just community. Elementary School Guidance and Counseling, 1975, 9, 299-308.

Gray, W.S., Gray oral reading tests. Indianapolis, Ind.: Bobbs-Merrill, 1963.

Grollman, E.A., Talking about death. Boston: Beacon Press, 1970.

Guerney, B.G., Jr. (Ed.), Psycho-therapeutic agents: New roles for non-professionals, parents and teachers. New York: Holt, Rinehart & Winston, 1969.

Guerney, B., Relationship enhancement: Skill-training programs for therapy, problem prevention, and enrichment. San Francisco: Jossey Bass, 1977.

Guerney, B., Stollack, G., & Guerney, L., The practicing psychologist as educator. Professional Psychology, 1971, 2, 276-282.

Guidance Associates of Pleasantville, New York. Understanding change in family: Not together anymore. New York: Author, 1973. Filmstrip.

Gumaer, J., Peer-facilitated groups. Elementary School Guidance and Counseling, 1972, 8, 4-11.

Gumaer, J., Training peer facilities. Elementary School Guidance and Counseling, 1976a, 11, 4-11.

Gumaer, J., Affective education through the friendship class. School Counselor, 1976b, 23, 257-263.

Gutwirth, S.W., You can learn to relax. Hollywood, Calif.: Wilshire, 1968.

Haley, J., Uncommon therapy. New York: Ballantine, 1973.

Hamburg, B., & Varenhorst, B., Peer counseling in the secondary schools: A community mental health project for youth. American Journal of Orthopsychiatry, 1972, 42, 566-581.

Hardy, R., & Cull, J., Social and rehabilitation services for the blind. Springfield, Ill.: Thomas, 1972.

Harris, D.B., Children's drawings as measures of intellectual maturity. New York: Harcourt, Brace & World, 1963.

Hauck, P., The rational management of children. Roslyn Heights, N.Y.: Libra, 1972.

Havighurst, R.J., Human development and education. New York: Longmans, Green, 1953.

Hemingway, P.D., The transcendental meditation primer: How to stop tension and start living. New York: Dell, 1975.

Hersch, C., From mental health to social action: Clinical psychology in historical perspective. American Psychologist, 1969, 24, 909-916.

Hittelman, R., Introduction to yoga. New York: Bantam, 1969.

Horne, A.M., Teaching parents a reinforcement program. Elementary School Guidance and Counseling, 1974, 9, 102-107.

Ilg, F.L., & Ames, L.B., School readiness. New York: Harper & Row, 1964.

Ivey, A.E. Microcounseling. Springfield, Ill.: Thomas, 1971.

Ivey, A.E., & Alschuler, A.S., An introduction to the field. Personnel and Guidance Journal, 1973, 51, 591-597.

Jacobson, E., You must relax. New York: McGraw-Hill, 1962.

James, M., & Jongeward, D., Born to win. Reading, Mass.: Addison-Wesley, 1971.

Jastak, J.F., & Jastak, S.R., The wide range achievement test. Wilmington, Del.: Guidance Associates, 1965.

Kanfer, F.H., & Saslow, G., Behavioral diagnosis. In Franks, C. (Ed.) Behavior Therapy: Appraisal and status. New York: McGraw-Hill. 1969. Pp. 417-444.

Kaplan, H.S., The illustrated manual of sex therapy. New York: Quadrangle, 1975.

Kater, D., & Spires, J., Biofeedback: The beat goes on. School Counselor, 1975, 23, 16-21.

Kazdin, A.E., Behavior modification in applied settings. Homewood, Ill.: Dorsey, 1975.

Keat, D., Anderson, S., Conklin, N., Elias, R., Faber, D., Felty, S., Gerba, J., Kochenash, J., Logan, W., Malecki, D., Martino, P., McDuffy, I., Schmerling, G., Schuh, C., & Selkowitz, L., Helping children to feel: A guide to affective curriculum materials for the elementary school. State College, Pa: The Counselor Education Press, 1972.

Keat, D.B., Fundamentals of child counseling. Boston: Houghton-Mifflin, 1974a.

Keat, D.B., Instructor's manual to accompany fundamentals of child counseling. Boston: Houghton-Mifflin, 1974b.

Keat, D.B., A reinforcement survey schedule for children. Psychological Reports, 1974c, 35, 287-293.

Keat, D., Bachman, P.F., Bates, E.K., Butler, R.G., Geier, D.M., Heller, A.J., Hoffman, L.A., Maki, K.D., Martin, D.E., Melpolder, P.H., Nace, C.A., Rapp, J.E., Roselle, J.M., Smith, P.L., Smyers, I.M., Speicher, M.C., Strong, R.R., & Trent, V., How can I help this child? University Park, Pa.: Cope Press, 1974.

Keat, D.B., Multimodal therapy with children: Two case histories. In A.A. Lazarus (Ed.), Multimodal behavior therapy, New York: Springer, 1976a. Pp. 116-132.

Keat, D.B., Multimodal counseling with children: Treating the BASIC ID. Pennsylvania Personnel and Guidance Association Journal, 1976b, 4, 21-25.

Keat, D.B., Training as multimodal treatment for peers. Elementary School Guidance and Counseling, 1976c, 11, 7-13.

Keat, D.B., Helping children feel good about themselves (tape 1). Harrisburg, Pa.: Professional Associates, 1977.

Keat, D.B., Self-relaxation program for children (tape 2). Harrisburg, Pa.: Professional Associates, 1977.

Keat, D.B., How to discipline children (tape 3). Harrisburg, Pa.: Professional Associates, 1977.

Keat, D.B., & Guerney, L.G., What every parent needs to know about raising children. University Park, Pa.: Cope Press, 1978.

Keat, D.B., & Hatch, E.J., Effective helping with learning disabled children. In S. Eisenberg & L.E. Patterson (Eds.), Helping clients with special concerns. Chicago: Rand McNally, in press.

Kelly, G.F., Mental imagery in counseling. Personnel and Guidance Journal. 1974, 53, 111-116.

Kern, R., & Kirby, J.H., Utilizing peer helper influence in group counseling. Elementary School Guidance and Counseling. 1971, 6, 70-75.

Kirk, S.A., McCarthy, J.J., & Kirk, W.D., Illinois test of psycholinguistic abilities. Urbana, Ill.: University of Illinois Press, 1968.

Knaus, W.J., Rational emotive education. New York: Institute for Rational Living, 1974.

Koeppen, A.S., Relaxation training for children. Elementary School Guidance and Counseling, 1974, 9, 14-21.

Knox, B., Marital happiness: A behavioral approach to counseling. Champaign, Ill.: Research Press, 1971.

Kohlberg, L., & Turiel, E., Moral development and moral education. In G. Lesser (Ed.), Psychology and educational process. Chicago: Scott, Foresman, 1971.

Koppitz, E.M., The Bender Gestalt test for young children. New York: Grune & Stratton, 1964.

Kramer, D., High school peer counseling. Personnel and Guidance Journal, 1974, 53, 330.

Kramer, E., Art as therapy with children. New York: Schocken, 1971.

Krumboltz, J.D., & Krumboltz, H.B., Changing children's behavior. Englewood Cliffs, N.J., Prentice-Hall, 1972.

Krumboltz, J.D., & Thoresen, C.E. (Eds.), Behavioral counseling: Cases and techniques. New York: Holt, Rinehart & Winston, 1969.

Krumboltz, J.D., & Thoresen, C.E. (Eds.), Counseling methods. New York: Holt, Rinehart & Winston, 1976.

Kuder, G.F., General interest survey, Form E. Chicago: Science Research Associates, 1971.

Lange, A.J., & Jakubowski, P., Responsible assertive behavior: Cognitive/ behavioral procedures for trainers. Champaign, Ill.: Research Press, 1976.

Lazarus, A.A., In support of technical eclecticism. Psychological Reports, 1967, 21, 415-416.

Lazarus, A.A., Daily living: Coping with tensions and anxieties. Relaxation exercises I, II, III (tapes). Chicago: Instructional Dynamics, 1970.

Lazarus, A.A., Behavior therapy and beyond. New York: Wiley, 1971.

Lazarus, A.A. (Ed.), Clinical behavior therapy. New York: Brunner/ Mazel, 1972.

Lazarus, A.A., Multimodal behavior therapy. Treating the "BASIC ID." The Journal of Nervous and Mental Disease, 1973, 156, 404-411.

Lazarus, A.A., Multimodal therapy: BASIC ID. Psychology Today, 1974a, 7, 59-63.

Lazarus, A.A., Multimodal behavioral treatment of depression. Behavior Therapy, 1974b, 5, 549-554.

Lazarus, A.A., The drug-free way to sleep soundly (tape). Valley Stream, N.Y.: Relaxation Dynamics, 1975.

Lazarus, A.A. (Ed.), Multimodal behavior therapy. New York; Springer, 1976.

Lazarus, A.A., Multimodal behavior therapy: Initial overview remarks. Workshop presented at the 54th Annual Meeting of the American Orthopsychiatric Association, New York, April 14, 1977.

Lazarus, A.A., In the mind's eye: The power of imagery therapy to give you control over your life. New York: Rawson, 1978.

Lazarus, A.A., & Fay, A., I can if I want to. New York: Morrow, 1975.

LeShan, L., How to meditate. New York: Bantam, 1974.

Lysebeth, A., Yoga self-taught. New York: Harper & Row, 1971.

Madsen, C., & Madsen, C.H., Parents/children/discipline. Boston: Allyn & Bacon, 1972.

Mahoney, M., Cognition and behavior modification. Cambridge, Mass.: Ballinger, 1974.

Mahoney, M., & Thoresen, C., Self control: Power to the person. Monterey, Calif.: Brooks/Cole, 1974.

Marquis, J.N., Morgan, W.G., & Piaget, G.W., A guidebook for systematic desensitization. (3rd Ed.) Palo Alto, Calif.: Veterans' Workshop, Veterans' Administration Hospital, 1973.

Mash, E.J., & Terdal, L.G. (Eds.), Behavior therapy assessment. New York: Springer, 1976.

Maslow, A., Motivation and personality. (2nd ed.) New York: Harper & Row, 1970.

Masters, W.H., & Johnson, V.F., Human sexual inadequacy. Boston: Little Brown, 1970.

Mayle, P., Robins, A., & Walter, P., What's happening to me? Secaucus, N.J.: Stuart, 1975.

McCann, B.G., Peer conseling: An approach to psychological education. Elementary School Guidance and Counseling, 1975, 9, 180-187.

McWilliams, S., & Finkel, N.J., High school students as mental health aids in the elmentary school setting. Journal of Consulting and Clinical Psychology, 1973, 40, 39-42.

Miller, L.C., Louisville behavior checklist for males, 6-12 years of age. Psychological Reports, 1967, 21, 885-896.

Morgan, C.T., & Deese, J., How to study. New York: McGraw-Hill, 1969.

Mosak, H.H., & Shulman, B.H., The life style inventory. Chicago: Alfred Adler Institute, 1971.

Myrick, R., & Moni, L., The counselor's workshop: Helping children disclose themselves. Elementary School Guidance and Counseling, 1972, 7, 55-59.

National Commission on Marihuana and Drug Abuse. Drug use in America: Problem in perspective. Washington, D.C.: U.S. Government Printing Office, March 1973. Stock No. 5266-00003.

Ornstein, R.E., The psychology of consciousness. San Francisco: Freeman, 1972.

Patterson, G.R., Families: Applications of social learning to family life. Champaign, Ill.: Research Press, 1971.

Patterson, G.R., & Gullion, M., Living with children. Champaign, Ill.: Research Press, 1968.

Perls, F.S., Gestalt therapy verbatim. Lafayette, Calif.: Real People Press, 1969.

Piers, E.V., & Harris, D.B., The Piers-Harris children's self concept scale. Nashville, Tenn.: Counselor Recordings and Tests, 1969.

Pomeroy, W., Boys and sex. New York: Delacorte, 1968.

Rashbaum-Selig, M., Assertive training for young people. School Counselor, 1976, 24, 115-122.

Reuben, D., The save-your-life diet. New York: Random House, 1975.

Riley, G.D., The Riley articulation and language test. Beverly Hills, Calif.: Western Psychological Services, 1966.

Rimland, B., High dosage levels of certain vitamins in the treatment of children with severe mental disorders. San Diego, Calif.: Institute for Child Behavior Research, 1968.

Rimm, D.C., & Masters, J.C., Behavior therapy: Techniques and empirical findings. New York: Academic Press, 1974.

Roach, E.G., & Kephart, N.C., The Purdue perceptual-motor survey. Columbus, Ohio: Merrill, 1966.

Robbins, J., & Fischer, D., Tranquility without pills: All about transcendental meditation. New York: Bantam, 1972.

Robertiello, R.C., Hold them very close, then let them go. New York: Dial Press, 1975.

Robinson, C.H., Normal and therapeutic nutrition. New York: Macmillan, 1972.

Rogers, C.R., Client-centered therapy. Boston, Mass.: Houghton-Mifflin, 1951.

Rosenberg, H., & Feldzamen, A., The doctor's book of vitamin therapy. New York: Putnam's, 1974.

Ross, A.O., Psychological disorders of children. New York: McGraw-Hill, 1974.

Rossman, H.M., & Kahnweiler, J.B., Relaxation training with intermeditate grade students. Elementary School Guidance and Counseling, 1977, 11, 259-266.

Russell, C., & Sipich, T., Cue controlled relaxation. Behavior Therapy, 1974, 5, 673-676.

Sax, S., & Hollander, S., Reality games. New York: Popular Library, 1972.

Schutz, W.C., Joy: Expanding human awareness. New York: Grove Press, 1967.

Schwarzrock, S., & Wrenn, C.G., My life -- What shall I do with it. Circle Pines, Minn.: American Guidance Service, 1973.

Simon, S., Howe, L., & Kirschenbaum, H., Values clarification. New York: Hart, 1972.

Simon, S., I am loveable and capable. Niles, Ill.: Argus Communications, 1973.

Skinner, B.F., & Krakower, S.A., Handwriting with write and see. Chicago: Lyons & Carnahan, 1968.

Slosson, R.L., Slosson intelligence test. East Aurora, N.Y.: Slosson Educational Publications, 1963.

Stanford, G., Methods and materials for death education. School Counselor, 1977, 24, 350-360.

Stevens, L.J., Stevens, G.E., & Stoner, R.B., How to feed your hyperactive child. New York; Doubleday, 1977.

Strandmark, J.F., Affect and cognition in drug education. In L. Abrams, E. Garfield, & J. Swisher (Eds.), Accountability in drug education. Washington, D.C.: Drug Abuse Council, 1973.

Stuart, R.B., & Davis, B., Slim chance in a fat world. Champaign, Ill.: Research Press, 1972.

Sulzer, B., & Mayer, G.R., Behavior modification procedures for school personnel. Hinsdale, Ill.: Dryden Press, 1972.

Tasto, D.L., & Hinkle, J.E., Muscle relaxation treatment for tension headaches. Behaviour Research and Therapy, 1973, 11, 347-349.

Terman, L.M., & Merrill, M.A., Stanford-Binet intelligence scale: Manual for the third revision, Form L-M. Boston: Houghton-Mifflin, 1960.

Thomas, E.J. (Ed.), Behavior modification procedure: A source book. Chicago: Aldine, 1974.

Thoresen, C.E., & Mahoney, M.J. Behavioral self control. New York: Holt, Rinehart & Winston, 1974.

U.S. Department of Agriculture. The thing the professor forgot. Pueblo, Colo.: Consumer Information, 1975.

Valett, R.E., The remediation of learning disabilities: A handbook of psychoeducational resource programs. Belmont, Calif.: Fearon, 1967.

Varenhorst, B.B., Training adolescents as peer counselors. Personnel and Guidance Journal, 1974, 53, 271-275.

Vogelsong, E.L., Preventive-therapeutic programs for mothers and adolescent daughters: A follow-up of relationship enhancement versus discussion and booster versus no-booster methods. Unpublished doctoral dissertation, The Pennsylvania State University, 1975.

Vriend, I.J., High-performing inner-city adolescents assist low-performing peers in counseling groups. Personnel and Guidance Journal, 1969, 47, 897-904.

Walker, C.E., Learn to relax. Englewood Cliffs, N.J.: Prentice-Hall, 1975.

Walkup, L.E., Creativity in science through visualization. Perceptual Motor Skills, 1965, 21, 35-41.

Watson, G., Nutrition and your mind. New York: Bantam, 1972.

Wechsler, D., Wechsler intelligence scale for children - revised. New York: Psychological Corporation, 1974.

Werry, J.S., & Quay, H.C., Exceptional Children, 1969, 35, 461-470.

Wilkinson, G.S., & Bleck, R.T., Children's divorce groups. Elementary School Guidance and Counseling, 1977, 11, 205-213.

Wolpe, J., The practice of behavior therapy. New York: Pergamon, 1969.

Wolpe, J., & Lang, P.J., Fear survey schedule. San Diego, Calif.: Educational and Industrial Testing Service, 1969.

Wolpe, J., & Lazarus, A.A., Behavior therapy techniques. New York: Pergamon, 1966.

Wrenn, C.G., & Schwarzrock, S., To like and be liked. Circle Pines, Minn.: American Guidance Service, 1970.

Wrenn, R.L., & Mencke, R., Students who counsel students. Personnel and Guidance Journal, 1972, 50, 687-689.

Yates, A.J., Behavior therapy. New York: Wiley, 1970.

Young, H.S., A rational counseling primer. New York: Institute for Rational Living, 1974.

Yudkin, J., Sweet and dangerous. New York: Bantam Books, 1972.

Zifferblatt, S., Improving study and homework behaviors. Champaign, Ill.: Research Press, 1970.

Author Index

Subject Index

About the Author

DONALD B. KEAT II is a Professor in the Graduate School at The Pennsylvania State University where he is primarily responsible for coordinating the child counseling program. In addition, he maintains a private practice in child therapy. He received his Ph.D. from Temple University. Dr. Keat has authored over 30 journal articles, written several invited chapters in books, developed audio cassettes and manuals for parents, produced a game for children, and has written five books.

TITLES IN THE PERGAMON GENERAL PSYCHOLOGY SERIES (Continued)